Party Lounge

the Ride is over!

By Mark Pondoff, AKA, Captain Marky Mark,
former Red Power Ranger

This book is sold subject to the condition that it shall not, by way of trade or otherwise, be lent, resold, hired out, or otherwise circulated without the publisher's prior consent in any form of binding or cover other than that in which it is published and without a similar condition including this condition being imposed on the subsequent purchaser.

The scanning, uploading, and distribution of this book via the Internet or via any other means without the permission of the publisher is illegal and punishable by law. Please purchase only authorized electronic editions and do not participate in or encourage electronic piracy of copyrighted materials. Your support of the author's rights is appreciated. All rights reserved under International and Pan-American Copyright Conventions.

Book Design: Felix Barca

Cover Design: Felix Barca

Editor: Lillian Nader

Text copyright © 2019 Mark Pondoff

All rights reserved.

ISBN: 978-0-578-52778-9

Table of Contents

PREFACE 5
The Travel Queen 9
The Pirate Hopper 20
The Ultra-Lounge 28
The Dream-Lounge 41
The Mega-Lounge Double-Decker 50
The Land Yacht 63
The Future Lounge 80
The Party Train 91
The Land Yacht 2.0 100
The Perfect Storm 112
My Lost TV Show 118
The TV Shows 122
Stupid Phone Calls and Illegal Party Buses 135
The End of an Era 148
Acknowledgments 155

Preface

My parents divorced when I was in the second grade. I lived with my mom in a huge house. All four of my older sisters had moved away after the divorce. My mom was gone all the time and I was like an emancipated minor. My uncle stepped in to raise me but was murdered a few years later. I was alone from second to sixth grades while my mom went through a mental breakdown. That's when, over the summer, I finally moved out of her house and in with my dad. I was scheduled to enter seventh grade. However, I felt as if I had to take control of my academics and so I asked to be placed in ninth grade. I visited La Serna High School and was given an aptitude test along with my transcript review from my prior parochial schools. After passing the tests, I was admitted as a freshman in 1984, going from sixth grade to ninth grade and completely skipping middle school.

I kept myself busy and found that my dad was gone even more than my mom was. Lots of people started assuming that his house was mine and that I lived there alone. Basically, that was correct, as I'd been on my own since grade school. I took care of myself in high school like a bachelor would. I did the grocery shopping, laundry, yard work, schoolwork, etc.

I acquired my bus building skills from experimenting with my mini truck in high school. Many people still remember

"Tricke." She was my dad's 1984 Nissan King Cab mini truck, which he handed down to me in 1986. In the 1980s everyone had a show truck. Because the competition was fierce to have the most modified truck in town, I taught myself to customize vehicles. Each week, my passion for customizing grew. I enjoyed coming up with new projects to create for the truck. Some of my ideas were absurd and extremely difficult to pull off. Looking back, I still don't know how I got any of it to work! It was trial and error as I taught myself without the help of the internet, which wasn't in existence at the time.

Many people criticized me, but I didn't care. I just kept creating, even if people thought it was silly or looked bad. Eventually, my ideas would become a reality, the result of taking a thought and conceptualizing it into a working prototype. My successful conversions were well worth all the drama I went through.

I was able to pacify my critics by having huge parties at my house. I won them over and rewarded myself at the same time! They didn't know it, but by charging them to get into my backyard parties, I was financing my truck projects! I quickly learned that throwing parties was fast and easy cash.

I had an after-school job, but it paid only minimum wage, which was $3.15 an hour. This wasn't going to do it for me, so I came up with my house party scheme. I circulated my "Pack the Back" party flyers around the high school and created so much hype that everyone felt it would help their reputations to be seen at my parties! I'd then charge a three-dollar-per-person admission fee. Once the backyard was packed to capacity, I'd call the cops and end the party! I had to give myself time to clean up and avoid any real damage to the property.

My dad found out about the parties when he came home unexpectedly during one of them! He was very mad at me until I handed him a huge wad of cash. You see, he had lost all his money that night in a poker game. That's why he had come home early. When I stuffed all that money into his front pocket, he turned and walked away. At that moment, we had an understanding.

We had a chicken coop with six birds. The next morning, my dad and I went to collect the eggs and we found that the hens were sitting on beer bottles. I turned to him and said, "Well, that's a party fowl!" We laughed so hard that we scared the birds!

I didn't realize it, but I excelled in entertaining back then. Setting the DJ and go-go dancers on the carport roof and turning it into a dance floor would make hundreds of dollars! This allowed me to quit my job.

The entertaining inspired me to take my show on the road with traveling parties. Mixing the truck with parties eventually led to a full party bus! "Tricke" was the name I gave my truck. It was also on my license plate. The cops were always pulling me over for fix-it tickets because the truck was so tricked-out. "Tricke" meant "Trick" as in "tricked out," and the "E" stood for "Extra" as in "Extra Tricked Out"! The name and reputation still live on in the minds of my classmates today!

Tricke was equipped with a modified airplane steering wheel. It was so cool! I eventually got a ticket for having it and so I had to change it back. The cop wasn't amused by it at all! The truck also had a channel top to make it convertible. A SnugTop camper shell covered the back, which housed a custom waterbed! I used to call it the "Stabbing Cabin." Tricke was a love machine, and me being a Scorpio ... well, let's just leave it at that!

There were two TVs—one in the cab and one in the back—along with a roof-mounted, limousine-style TV antenna, VCR, CB, PA system, musical horn, and 1,000-watt stereo with two 15-inch subwoofers that shook the cars next to me in traffic! I had special "Knight Rider"-styled red Cylon lights installed in the front grill. I custom-made a small windshield wiper for the rear camper shell's back window. In 1984 there were no rear windshield wipers on any vehicle!

The truck was lowered, with custom rims and a shirt kit all around it. I whited out the truck so it looked European. It had a special exterior. Tricke and I got into lots of trouble, creating a legendary status that lives on today! Lights on the outside made it stand out. The Whittier P.D. must have had a party the day we moved out of town!

My continued journey from a mini truck to rolling monoliths has inspired others to follow their dreams. I set the template with my "No quit, take no shit" attitude, making this world my minion!

I now enjoy retirement at 48, and my second life has just begun!

The Travel Queen

The Travel Queen had been our family coach since 1973. My dad was an avid poker player and would go missing for days at a time. One week my dad showed up in our driveway in the Travel Queen instead of his Cadillac. We all came outside to watch my mom berate him.

"Where is your car?" she yelled.

My dad had an audience consisting of all five kids and the nosy neighbors. He'd been gone for nearly two days straight. My mom's fear was that he had lost his Cadillac in a poker game.

My dad looked tired and disheveled as he finally got in a word. "Bertha, I won the damn thing in a poker game!"

To my mom's relief, we all had a good laugh. I instantly boarded the Travel Queen for the first time and fell in love with my new motor home. This would be a lifelong friendship between man and machine!

The little RV had made many family memories. One of them was its very first party RV gig! One of my four sisters was to be married at our house. My mom wanted no liquor at the wedding. However, my dad had other plans. He stocked the Travel Queen full of booze, drove it to our house, and parked it in front of the wedding venue as a mobile bar. It took only a short time for a line to form at the rear window. My dad, acting as a bartender, was pushing drinks through the small opening when my mom came outside.

Bertha screamed, "Nick, what the hell are you doing? This was to be a dry wedding!"

My dad quickly closed the window and released the parking brake as though it were a ship's anchor, then sailed down the street! He came back a few hours later and my mom ordered the staff to place the wedding garbage inside the RV. My dad had failed to lock the door and was unaware of my mom's nefarious plan. Later that evening, Bertha's plan would backfire, as the Travel Queen was to be my bedroom for the night. She forgot that I'd given up my bedroom for my cousins, who were there for the wedding. Being a little captain back then, I made my way over all the garbage bags and went to bed in the back of the coach. It seems, for me, "No good deed goes unpunished!" This would be one of many memories for me and the Travel Queen.

Eventually, it was the end of the line for the Travel Queen and my dad. The RV served as a hotel for him when my parents got divorced. My dad had told me that he considered the Travel Queen to be a family heirloom. Eventually, he was no longer capable of caring for her. The Travel Queen remained parked at his house in Whittier, California, untouched for years.

After a very long ten years of owning and operating Mark's Handyman Service, I needed a change. At the time, I lived in Huntington Beach, California. I decided to take a brief break from being self-employed and took a job with a plumbing company in Santa Ana, California. I was there for approximately six months.

One day, I was heading into work when my truck broke down. The truck was going to be in the shop for a while due to transmission failure. I called my dad and asked if I could use the Travel Queen. When I went to pick it up, it wouldn't start, and someone had been living it! My dad was in his seventies at the time and had no idea what was going on out front where the RV was parked.

He agreed to give me the coach and I promised to never sell her. He signed the RV over to me and I started the salvaging process. This was to be a big undertaking. The Travel Queen hadn't had any maintenance for over a decade. All of that was about to change as I eagerly got started.

Excited about what I'd find after all these years, I took my first steps inside, expecting to be flooded by instant memories of the past. Instead, I dealt with foul smells of the present! I could see that we'd had a tenant—and not the four-legged kind. It was human!

The mess left by the transient who was living inside was considerable. It looked as if a party bomb had gone off. The smell of puke and feces permeated the interior. I had to visit the local hardware store to gather up a makeshift bio-hazard suit! After a few days of clean-up and trash removal, it was time to focus on the engine.

It refused to start, just as I expected. First, I charged the battery and checked the spark plugs. I removed the air cleaner so it could breathe. It seemed as if nothing could coax the engine into starting. Finally, I tried some fresh fuel injected directly into the carburetor. The small Dodge 318 engine started sputtering back to life. With white clouds of smoke puffing out of the tailpipes, the Travel Queen was resurrected! My trip to Whittier turned out to be a rescue and recovery mission. There would be many more to come in the future for PartyLounge.

I was departing from my dad's place in Whittier to get the Travel Queen back to Huntington Beach, but would she make it? The RV was in terrible shape! The generator wouldn't come online. The tires were bald, and the wiring had been chewed by a rat that was also living inside rent-free!

The ride was rough, as the shocks were blown out. I'd never driven a stagecoach, but I imagined this was about as close as you could get. The exhaust was leaking and I was getting smoked out. The alignment was off by a mile and the coach pulled hard to the right. It took a lot of muscle work to keep the RV in its lane.

I had made it halfway home when the rat living in the back decided to come out and pay me a visit! I swerved to the far-right lane and parked in a bus stop. I retrieved the broom left over from the cleanup and quickly opened the door. My plan was to push him out gently. As I started chasing the rat around the coach, I heard an extremely loud honk from a city bus behind me. I could tell the driver was very upset, as I was in her loading zone. She came out of her bus and up to the now-open door. That's when the rat jumped out and almost landed in her arms. The bus driver shrieked and she ran back to her bus! There was only one thing left for me to do: put the Travel Queen back into gear and floor it! Luckily for me, the license plate had fallen off several miles back due to all the road vibrations!

I was entering my hometown when the exhaust pipe gave way and hit the ground, emitting a very loud blast, like that of a shotgun. The sound caused all the pedestrians sitting on a bus bench to hit the pavement! They thought it was a drive-by shooting. I drove away, leaving a curtain of sparks in my wake!

I was pulling down my street, thinking the worst of it was behind me. Well, it sure was, because the RV's septic tank had also burst during the trip. The main drain broke away from its support, allowing the street to do the rest. It opened up the tank and all the sewage started leaking out. The RV was full of sewage that had been generated by the bum living inside it. The smell got worse at every stop. By the time I got into my driveway, the tank was empty, which explained why people were honking and yelling at me. I'd been wondering why their windshield wipers were on.

I thought to myself, 'Man, those people are crazy!'

Mechanical repairs started the next day. It took a few months to get the Travel Queen road-worthy.

Back then, my fiancée Mikki and I were planning our wedding in Mexico. For over a year, we had made multiple trips back and forth from the U.S. Our big day came, and we used the Travel Queen to take us to Mexico. She would have a myriad of tasks besides transporting us there. The coach was to serve as a dressing room, storage, and accommodations. The venue for the wedding was The Cliff House, just outside of Rosarito Beach. When we arrived, I found my guests out front, swimming in the hotel's fountain. It was a hot day and there was no pool. After several shots of tequila, they made the executive decision that the fountain would do!

This day had it all! My mom, Bertha, drove up in her Mercedes and wanted me to park her car, take her bags, and check her in. I was flustered and busy at the time, trying to get my drunk friends out of the hotel fountain! My fiancée was in the room getting ready when her hairdryer blew out the hotel's circuit and we had no way of resetting it. I quickly remedied the situation by running an extension cord from the Travel Queen to our room. Thank God I'd fixed the generator.

The ceremony was a comedy of errors as my half-drunk friends baked in the sun, waiting for the preacher, who was 45 minutes late. When he finally arrived, my guests were passing out. To make matters worse, the preacher kept calling me by the wrong name. Our ceremony had all the makings of a low-budget comedy film! The food, drinks, and accommodations had all been bait-and-switch on us.

Later that night, as we came back from the wedding reception, we found that our room's electricity still hadn't been repaired. However, we made the best of it. I managed to rig a light from the Travel Queen in our room. The little coach would prove to be invaluable again.

In the morning, I had words with the hotel manager, expressing my complaints. He offered free breakfast for our trouble. I told him a meal wasn't going to make up for ruining our wedding! When we left the hotel, my only recourse was to let the septic tank go in the parking lot! Hey, what can I say? Shit happens!

The next week, it was back to work at my plumbing job. My truck was still in the shop, so T.Q. would have to get me to and from work. I spent my lunchtimes in the coach, as my breaks were very short. I liked to lie down in the back and rest. I was thinking to myself about what kind of business I should start next. The plumbing job was hard manual labor and didn't pay much. I really couldn't see myself doing it as a career. Just then, I had an epiphany! I was thinking about how cool it would be to drive T.Q. around like a taxi or limo. "Hmmm, but how could it be done?"

I drove home that night and started brainstorming the possibilities. I told my wife about my idea, and she said, "Nobody is going to rent that thing!"

However, I remained undeterred. This would be the push I needed to prove her wrong! I thought, *Someday she'll owe me a retraction*. That was wishful thinking, as I'm still waiting!

With testicular fortitude and blind faith, I set out to start my next business. I called my boss and put in my two-week notice. The renovations started after I'd completely left my job. I remember being curbside and shoving things out the door of the motor home. My nosey neighbors were watching me with curiosity as I gutted the coach. One neighbor in particular (let's call her Ms. Crabbits) was watching my every move from her kitchen window. Because I had an audience, my thought was to put on a show. So, I took a small seat cushion off the sofa and lit it on fire. Then I threw it out the door. I jumped out of the RV and put it out with my shoes. I was stomping on it like a wild man. I went back inside the coach to keep working as I laughed my azz off. Five minutes later, the fire department showed up. Guess the joke was on me!

The pile of debris was building up and it was time to haul it away. I decided to leave it out for the night, as the neighborhood harvesters would take what they wanted. Just as I figured, the next morning, only half the pile remained. The coach was a blank slate now. Only the driver seat was left. I contemplated what I was going to do with the interior.

At that time, there was no internet, so my options were limited. I visited the mall looking for some cool lights. I found two lamps at the electronic store. One lamp said "*Party*" and the other said "*Lounge.*" I put the two lamps together to form one word. I then mounted the sign in the coach. I liked the word so much; it was then that I decided "PartyLounge" would be the name of my new business. I renamed the Travel Queen, "The Pirate Hopper," and gave it a themed interior to match. It had a slot machine, liquor on tap, a dance pole, and pirate-themed upholstery.

My first RV-to-party-bus conversion was now complete. There were no other RV party buses at the time. I'd put PartyLounge signs on the sides of the coach, and I quickly started getting jobs. Ms. Crabbits noticed the Hopper coming and going and decided to make trouble for me. She was a police dispatcher for LGB, or Long Beach Airport. As such, she was able to convince the police department that I was running an illegal gambling and brothel on wheels! None of this was true; however, this lady could sound convincing.

The police came out to investigate the Pirate Hopper and me. They threatened to shut me down and impound the coach if they saw me on the road. My neighbor even got the Pirate Hopper towed for being parked on the street. It seemed my new business was finished before it began. I fought to get my coach back and hashed it out with the police. They told me to get a limousine license and insurance. At that time, no such licensing for an RV-to-party-bus conversion existed.

I called the California Public Utilities Commission to inquire about compliance. However, like many state agencies, they were useless—just there to take our money while not doing their jobs! I continued to operate in defiance, with my "nobody tells me what to do" attitude in full force. I had a friend in the limousine business, and he gave me a number to call. My application was on the way. I filled it out and sent in a check. They never bothered to inspect my vehicle. I got my limousine license and insurance, then headed to the police department to prove that I was legit!

I got the Pirate Hopper back on the road. This time, she was carrying my sexy waitresses as a bonus to the rental experience. The girls were recruited from my neighborhood and loved to get paid to party. Ms. Crabbits saw the scantily clad women load my coach several times a week and got super jealous. Turns out she had a thing for me! I tried to befriend her and keep the peace, but this wasn't to be. As a gesture of peace, I even built shelves in her garage for free. However, Ms. Crabbits was a gun-toting, cat-loving shut-in who was hell-bent on my destruction. She had the local H.O.A, Homeowners Association, up my ass as well as the police, the city code enforcers, and anyone else she could recruit to mess with me! Things were getting pretty sketchy in the hood. She even took the lug nuts off my wife's car, causing the tire to fly off. Luckily, my wife wasn't hurt. We couldn't prove that Ms. Crabbits was the culprit, as she had the sympathy of the local P.D. We sold our house and got out of there, hoping this would be the last we saw of her. However, she managed to locate my new home. One day, I saw her drive by my house. Shortly thereafter, she filed a restraining order against me.

It was clear that this lady was nuts! Our day in court was a three-ring circus. I was accused of everything she could make up but she had no proof. I anticipated my character assassination, so I brought a full contingent of witnesses who testified on my behalf. Ms. Crabbits was chastised and berated by the judge, who was less than happy with her for wasting the court's time. The judge ruled in my favor and threw her out of court. The courtroom of strangers erupted in applause for me as if I'd just hit the winning home run! Ms. Crabbits was finally out of our lives! However, she wouldn't be the last of my stalkers.

As the money started rolling in, I was able to improve the Pirate Hopper. She got a new paint job and graphics, one of which featured my photo, on the sides. It was a picture of me holding my favorite cognac on a rooftop bar in Vegas. It was fun having my street credit and it inspired me to work hard. PartyLounge was growing into a real transportation company.

The Pirate Hopper

Once the Travel Queen had been transformed into the Pirate Hopper, it was time to put her to work. One of my first big paying jobs was a family who requested a seaside picnic. The Pirate Hopper still had an oven and stove in it at the time. The lady was very nice and asked if she could bring her poodle. I said yes, as I was under the impression that it was a small dog. As luck would have it, when I pulled up to their home, a giant horse-like animal called a Standard Poodle was out front, waiting to board! As my party bus quickly turned into Noah's Ark, I thought to myself, *I hope this animal is housebroken!* The dog's name was Zeus. Zeus seemed more interested in riding with me than with his family and sat next to the driver's seat. As I tried to steer, he would nudge my arms with his enormous head to garner more affection. The family seemed clueless about the situation Zeus was creating. I tried to push him away, but the dog wouldn't take the hint. He jumped into my lap, completely blocking my field of vision! That was when the lady took the love-sick canine to the back. Thank God we didn't crash! What would I have told the police? "Officer, actually, the dog was the one that was driving!"

I found a beautiful spot in Corona Del Mar, overlooking the ocean. I parked on the street and the family got out. The lady was impressed with my driving skills and I hoped her tip would reflect that! They'd brought food and I was expecting them to take it to the picnic area of the park. She then told me to start heating the lasagna. I was like, "What?" It turned out that she expected me to be the chef, too! It was my first $115-per-hour gig, so I just did it.

The cooking consisted of heating up things. I was doing a fine job when a knock came on the door. It was the neighbor from across the street. She was one of those snotty, ultra-rich, entitled, lost-with-reality, I-married-rich-guy types. She commanded me to move the Hopper and threatened to call the cops. She stood in the street, yelling at me. I thought to myself, *I can't be the first person to park here on this very busy street with a park overlooking the ocean, so what is this lady's problem? Logic dictates that if you buy a house near an airport, you're going to hear some noise and see planes!*

Dismayed by her lack of couth and class, and by her vulgar demeanor, I promptly told her to piss off and then continued to cook. The police showed up in minutes as if this were the biggest thing to happen in their town. They began to harass me, and a small melee ensued. As the neighbor, police, and I started yelling at one another, my clients and Zeus ran over to defend me. This was turning out to be quite the picnic! We were all allowed to leave without further incident. As I pulled off the curb, I drove by the troublesome neighbor and flipped her the bird while tooting the horn! I took the clients home after I found another spot where they could finish their lunch. At the drop-off, they all shook my hand and told me I'd done a good job.

As I started the engine, I was relieved that the afternoon's gig was over. It turned out that I wasn't the only one to be relieved onboard. The family didn't tip me but Zeus did. In the back of my coach was a nice, steamy pile on the floor. I contemplated leaving it on the troublesome neighbor's driveway! However, going straight home sounded better. With time to reflect on what had just happened, I realized that my rental contract needed more rules, starting with "no pets!"

A BASEBALL GAME AND THE BANGERS

The Pirate Hopper was rented for a baseball game in Los Angeles. My clients had to be picked up in a less-than-favorable neighborhood but I took the job anyway. By now, experience was telling me not to service this area but I thought, *What the hell, the money is good!*

We pulled into the stadium and the clients started a tailgating party around my coach. That was all fine and dandy until some hood rats rolled up on us and started hitting on my clients' girlfriends. At first, I thought they knew each other. When the girls refused their advances, the bangers focused on stealing my clients' alcohol. It was obvious that I had no choice but to intervene. I asked the bangers to leave but they weren't going without a fight. Being a former Power Ranger, I drop-kicked one of them in the head and he flew out the door. Another banger was hit by a passenger from behind with a beer bottle. The rest of the bangers bailed out to regroup. Seeking revenge, one banger tried to get back on board without his backup. This was a big mistake, as I put the coach into gear and he fell out of it. He then tried to run us down on foot. I brake-checked him and he ran into the back bumper. I then floored the Pirate Hopper as someone closed the door! We made a clean getaway and parked on the other side of the stadium. To my amazement, no police or security were there to see any of this! Today, if you visit that same stadium, you can't tailgate and the police are everywhere! It's like visiting a prison camp!

HEAVY METAL CONCERT ROBBERY

The Pirate Hopper's next adventure was at a heavy metal concert in Riverside. The RV had been rented out by some of my old high school friends. I knew almost everyone on board, and they had a ticket for me. I was going to get paid to attend a concert! Wow, this business had its perks! I thought this was going to be an easy and fun gig. Well, it started out that way. I'd arrived at the pickup location for the twelve passengers when I noticed the mob on the curb. Twenty-three people were waiting to get onboard. Not knowing any better, I took every one of them! They were packed in like sardines. We got to the concert and, while I was parking, a fight broke out in the back. My friends were already drunk and two of them had just punched each other. I went from driver to referee in an instant! Fortunately, I was able to defuse the liquor-infused situation.

When we entered the concert, the animosity continued. I spent most of my time as a bodyguard for the one friend who couldn't seem to stay out of trouble. I got to enjoy the last part of the show, as he finally passed out on the grass. At the end of the concert, other friends helped us drag him to the exit. He finally got on his feet again and was ready to fight! We got him to the Pirate Hopper, where he was administered another beer. That finally KO'd him!

While driving back, I noticed we were low on gas. I pulled into a gas station. To my surprise, everyone got out and headed into the convenience store. As I fueled the Pirate Hopper, I noticed passengers running out of the store with liquor. I asked one of them, "What's going on?"

Just then, the clerk came out, shouting at all of us. Turns out the passengers had just robbed the store of alcohol.

They explained that because the clerk had been on the phone and couldn't be bothered to ring them up, they'd gotten angry and decided to run out the door. Thinking I was going to be implicated, I took swift action. Like an episode of Indiana Jones, I started the engine and got out of there!

After a long drive and rattled nerves, we arrived at the drop-off. Just when I thought it was over, two of my drunkest passengers hopped on the front bumper and tried to ride the Hopper down the street. They were holding onto the windshield wipers. I tried to shake them off by turning on the wipers. The guys promptly snapped off the wiper arms as I came to a screeching halt! I got out and pulled them off the bumper, then made them walk home. The damages to the Hopper were minimal but the lesson I learned was priceless! Don't rent to friends, don't overload the coach, and hire security!

The Pirate Hopper's next assignment was at The Key Club in Hollywood. Every Monday, a regular customer, whom we called Mr. Big, rented the Pirate Hopper to see his favorite band, "Metal School." Mr. Big got his name because he was extremely arrogant, cheap, and clearly on steroids. He liked women, booze, and heavy metal. He always wanted me to bring the waitresses.

Hollywood is a very difficult town to drive a big vehicle in, and there's no parking anywhere. Mr. Big always wanted to be front-doored, which posed a problem, as there's no parking on Sunset Boulevard. I ended up doing it anyway, hoping for a better tip. I had to block a lane of Sunset Boulevard while they hopped off. For my efforts, no better tip was to be had. The meter readers loved chasing me around town. They followed me all over, trying to write me a ticket! Eventually, I found a market and parked there.

When the concert was over, I swooped in to pick them up. A cab driver took issue with me, as he wanted the last space at the curb. I honked at him and told him to get bent. He got out of his car and started pounding on my window. I grabbed my client's beer and sprayed him with it. Mr. Big and the girls hadn't boarded yet and were nowhere in sight. There were no cell phones back then, and I was on borrowed time! The cab driver retrieved a tire iron and was about to cause some serious damage to the Hopper. I sped off, and the chase was on.

I was going west on Sunset, which took me right into Beverly Hills. I sped through the small streets of the neighborhood. There was very little room in which to maneuver, with cars parked on either side of the street. The cab driver had caught up to me and I brake-checked him. Then I floored it again, hitting a dip in the road. The RV flew into the air and "YES," it was airborne! The septic tank valve opened upon landing. Everything came spilling out and covered the cabbie, who had just driven through the mess. The cabbie stopped in disbelief as I continued driving away. I picked up my clients and told them what had just happened. Turns out they were too drunk to believe me. I told them the bathroom was out of order for the night, and I had to lock the door!

When I got them to the drop-off, one waitress went into Mr. Big's home. Being super tired and in no mood to wait, we left her there! I found out she slept with him. She called me the next day demanding her pay. I told her she wasn't getting paid to sleep with my clients. She threatened me and turned into a psycho.

NOTE: *The Pirate Hopper has been remodeled and is now my Personal Party Bus. She is parked on a private driveway at my home. We use her all the time. We have a driver on staff who takes us to outings that are not suitable for rideshare applications.*

The Ultra-Lounge

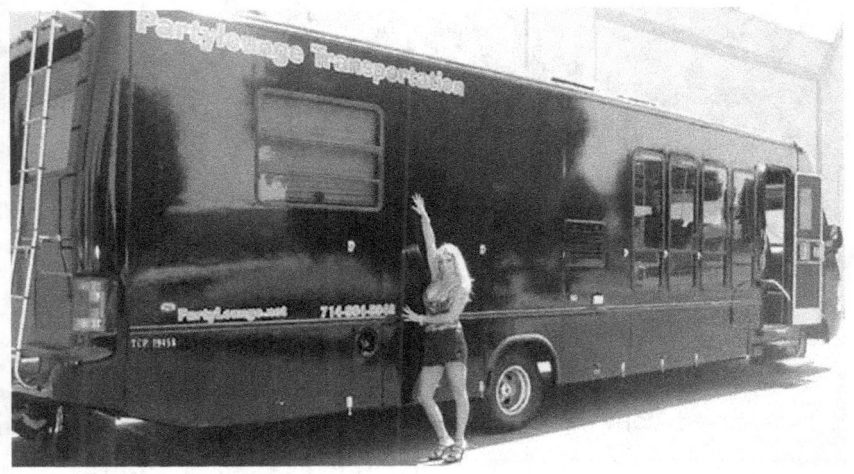

The Pirate Hopper was doing very well despite all the crazy adventures! I managed to save enough money to buy another RV. I wanted to create another themed party bus. I looked all over Southern California for my next coach.

Upon arriving at Travel Land, USA, I spotted a coach parked behind the building, with just the nose sticking out. It was a Ford Ultra Sport. That's how the name Ultra-Lounge came to me. It was a derivative of the original name. I put together the words and dropped Sport. The Ultra-Lounge was born.

The coach had many windows, like a limousine, and I knew it was going to be a perfect fit! I'd learned a lot from my first RV-to-party-bus conversion. I was eager to get started, and I had lots of great ideas for the new project. Gutting this coach was more work because Ultra-Lounge was two times bigger than the Pirate Hopper.

Ultra would have a leopard-print interior and a V.I.P. room in the back, with a dance pole. There was also a dance pole in the main cabin. The bathroom had an L-shaped bench while the bar had a commercial-grade well, just like a real bar. She was a beauty! After operating the Pirate Hopper and Ultra-Lounge together at some concerts, I was noticed by *Orange Coast Magazine.* They contacted me and wanted an interview for an article. My wife and I were happy and flattered to do it. This was the first time, outside of my commercial, that I got free press.

LADDER SURFING THROUGH NEWPORT

Ultra's first gig was to bar-hop in Newport Beach, California. I was the driver and had the waitress, Natty, with me. She was one of my first party dolls and always went with me when I drove. Sometimes she brought her friends.

Party Lounge - The Ride is over!

Passengers loved to have the bus full of pretty young girls. The girls got a free ride and made tips off my passengers. They often got invited into venues and sometimes we even had free dinners.

As we were en route to Sharkeez to pick up our clients, Natty decided to have a drink. At that time, she liked to loosen up prior to meeting everyone. I didn't mind, as I wanted her to be as friendly as possible with the guests. Natty could hold her liquor and even, on occasion, drink some of the male guests under the table!

The bus ran over a very large pothole and Natty spilled her drink all over her top. I was unaware of what was happening as I continued to drive. She decided the best way to remedy the situation was to take off her top and place it in the microwave. Part of the kitchen, including a working microwave, remained in the RV party bus. However, you can't dry clothes in the microwave! Doing this quickly blew out half the circuits in the bus. As I drove down the street, I noticed everything went dark inside the bus. I called back to Natty: "What the hell is going on? What happened to the lights?"

Natty said, "Marky, you're going to be so mad at me! I'm so sorry!"

I pulled over and saw that the back cabin was completely dark. Not one light was on and the stereo didn't work. I was freaking out because we were moments away from picking up the clients. Without the interior limousine lights or stereo, she was no longer a party bus! I frantically tried to remedy the situation but had no tools onboard. How would I diagnose what had caused the loss of power? That's when Natty confessed that she had tried to dry her clothes in the microwave and we had blown a circuit.

Figuring that the microwave was on a ground fault circuit interrupter (commonly known as GFCI), I started searching the bus for this receptacle. These are the same kinds of receptacles you find in your bathroom next to the sink. Press the reset button and the power will come back on; at least that's what I was hoping. The clock was ticking and I didn't want to be late picking up the clients, who were now calling me and asking where the bus was. I still had 15 minutes to get there, I explained, and was stuck at a light. However, they had no idea that the party bus was sidelined and parked a few streets over. I started going to all the receptacles, looking for the GFCI, and finally found one in the bathroom. I quickly reset it. To my delight, the lights came back on in the bathroom. However, the rest of the bus was still in the dark. The next GFCI was found under the bar sink. Using the light from my telephone, I reset it, too. The rest of the bus came back to life, much to my relief!

I picked up the group of young passengers at Sharkeez Bar without incident. The evening was going great! Ultra-Lounge was equipped with an operable back window and ladder. I labeled the window, "Emergency Exit." I thought this would be a great safety feature.

With all the passengers on board, I started making my way out of the club parking lot. I was going slowly because Ultra-Lounge was 36 feet long. I noticed people yelling and waving at me as we drove by. I thought they were complimenting me on the party RV, so I just kept going.

As I was rolling down Pacific Coast Highway in Newport Beach, a motorcycle cop came roaring up to my driver's side window.

"Pull over!" he yelled.

I wondered how long he had been chasing me. I pulled over to the curb and he ran to the back of the coach. I was thinking, *How strange; what's he doing back there?* I got out of the coach to go see. The officer was helping a half-dressed female passenger off the back ladder. She had missed the party RV and had run to catch up with us, then jumped onto the back ladder. As we were going down the street, she had ridden the ladder while the drunk people on board were trying to pull her through the back window. But she wouldn't let go of it. She was terrified! I estimated she might have been holding on for half a mile!

I can't imagine what this looked like to all the spectators on the curb. However, it must have been hilarious to witness! I explained to the cop that I had no idea she was back there. He let us all go! I shook my head in disbelief, as I thought we were all going to jail and that the coach would be impounded. I swiftly pulled away before he changed his mind!

A MISSING NEW YEAR'S EVE BUS

New Year's Eve is one of the most difficult and dangerous nights to be on the road, especially in a bus full of drunk people. The last time I drove on New Year's Eve, I had a waitress go with me. We witnessed countless accidents, solo spin-outs, and people who drove their cars straight off the highway. Cars were on fire and stuck everywhere. The freeways looked like a war zone. My waitress got so drunk, she became part of the problem; I was stuck babysitting her and the passengers.

Due to my past experiences with New Year's Eve, I opted out of driving. Delegating this task to my staff turned out to be a huge mistake! I can't mention my driver's name, so let's call him "Donkey." The coach was booked to full capacity, so I also hired a security guard. I can't tell you his name either. We'll call him "Dummy."

Donkey and Dummy had worked on my buses before, so I thought they could handle this gig. I was out with my wife at a local beach bar, waiting to ring in the new year. I kept my phone on vibrate, as I was always on red alert when the coaches were out without me present.

The call I'd been hoping to avoid came in, and my heart skipped a beat. I looked down at the screen. It was my driver. The coach had broken down in Los Angeles. As I was trying to remedy the situation, my phone was flooded with calls from the passengers. All were intoxicated and extremely difficult to deal with. They acted as if we'd planned the breakdown.

The next morning, I called my driver to find out where he'd left the bus so I could have it towed. This was when the real trouble started. To my disbelief, he had no idea where he'd left the bus! He explained that during the chaos of the evening, he'd just bailed out with the passengers who had all gotten cab rides. I then called the security guard. He had no clue where the bus was either! Back then, there were no tracking devices for vehicles, so I called the LAPD. They hadn't seen it either.

By now, I was irate! How do you lose a 36-foot black bus with my photo, the company name and logo, and the words "Ultra-Lounge" written all over it?

I called the police tow yards in L.A., thinking maybe they'd taken it. Nope, they hadn't seen it either. It took the LAPD a full week to locate my bus. What an expensive night! I had to refund the passengers, then get the bus towed and repaired. Donkey and Dummy took no responsibility for their actions and were less than sympathetic about the loss of the coach. They neither offered up an apology nor offered to help me find it. In the end, their indifference and poor judgment were too much of a liability for me. They wanted to be paid for the entire night but Donkey and Dummy were fired and never worked for me again. They were the first crew members to be fired from the PartyLounge, but more would follow! Crossing the Captain is biting the hand that feeds! This is a lesson I had to teach many ungrateful, arrogant, ignorant, non-couplable, and jealous employees.

THE NO CLASS HIGH ROLLER

One day started off with a frantic early-morning call from the owner of a mortgage company. He was very full of himself!

He mentioned that his pickup was in a very affluent and expensive part of Orange County, California called Newport Coast—as if I'd never heard of this community or that I should be impressed. At this point, I wasn't sure what to think. My experience with this elite demographic has always been challenging. Just the pickup process alone is difficult. They live atop very steep hills in gated communities, which is a real problem for buses.

The entrances and streets weren't designed for such large vehicles. From our phone conversations, I could tell that this guy was going to be difficult. However, despite my gut telling me to ditch this lead, I decided to take the gig. The bills had to be paid! I was in for an evening to remember!

For the sake of anonymity, we'll call this client "The Juice." He frantically explained that his reservation with a limousine company had been canceled. He was having a corporate party in a few hours and needed a 15-passenger coach. He also wanted a cocktail waitress. I gave him a price of $125 per hour, including the waitress. I explained that tips weren't included and he assured me that we'd be well taken care of. He said that he used limousines all the time, so we'd get a lot of business from him. For that reason, he wanted the bus at a cheaper price. This guy was a real tool! He needed me in a few hours and wanted a discount! I wanted to back out and I hadn't even finished the call yet. It was apparent to me why the first limousine company had canceled on him!

While en route to the pickup destination, I warned Waitress Natty to be extra vigilant with the primary, as he seemed to be difficult. As soon as we arrived at the pickup, the primary earned his name, "The Juice." This is my nickname for guys who are obviously jacked up on steroids. He was wearing a super-tight shirt with the buttons down low enough to show his man cleavage.

I greeted him and his wife and introduced myself and the waitress. His wife snubbed us. She looked like an ad for every makeup store in the mall! Throughout the night, I had to continually remind them what our names were, as they preferred to call us "Boy and Girl." Yes, they were condescending, rude pricks!

Mr. J's guests arrived, and he had double the number of people he'd told me! We had 30 passengers onboard! He chose to visit a bar in Laguna Beach, a very bad city to drive buses in. The streets are very tight with hills, and some are one-way. There's literally nowhere to pull over and park.

His first stop was a restaurant/bar on the very busy Pacific Coast Highway. There was no way to drop off him and his 30 guests at this location without blocking a lane of traffic and risking a ticket. This type of ticket is called "Impeding the follow of traffic" and it's a moving violation. Commercial-licensed drivers are not allowed traffic school. I'd gotten this ticket before in a similar situation in Los Angeles ... and on the same bus! The officer couldn't care less about the difficulties I was facing onboard and was happy to write me the ticket! I explained to Mr. J that we couldn't stop on PCH. He apparently didn't like the word "no" and got in my face. Despite my better judgment, and wanting to keep the primary happy, I stopped on PCH and dropped them off. Cars were honking and it was pandemonium on the curb. His group wasn't exiting but, rather, trying to finish their drinks even after Natty and I told them to get off ASAP! The police drove by and were about to turn around when I finally managed to get the last person out and sped off! Wow, that was close! I found a parking spot five blocks away.

Natty and I had just started cleaning the coach when The Juice called to be picked up already! He wanted us to take him two blocks from where they were. I tried in vain to explain why we couldn't risk picking them up on PCH again. I said they'd either have to walk the five blocks to the coach or simply walk the two blocks to the next bar, where I could pick them up when they were ready.

He started yelling through the phone at me because he expected to be "front-doored" at each location. I guess he should have chosen a smaller vehicle or a bigger town! He didn't understand the laws of physics! Big bus, little streets! I picked up him and his miscreant crew at bar two and they were all mad at us.

Their next destination was bar three and, yes, it was in the same town! I went back to my parking spot, which luckily was still open. I told The Juice that they'd have to walk to bar three. That's when the roid rage started. Guys on steroids are typically hostile, and he was no exception.

The Juice got into my face as if he was going to attack me. He then proceeded to berate me in front of everyone. His wife decided to join in, stating that she could drive the coach better than I could. She then bragged that they owned an RV that was even bigger than the Ultra-Lounge.

I managed to keep my cool and stepped off the coach. Shocked at what had just happened, I regained my composure and went back on board. The Juice and his wife had started in on Natty, addressing her as "Girl." I reminded them what her name was, and they addressed me as "Boy."

The obnoxious couple then came back up to the cockpit and told me to drive them to Las Vegas. I laughed at them and said, "NO WAY!" They seemed shocked!

Simultaneously, they pulled out large rolls of money and said, "Nonsense! You're not getting a tip!"

I said, "You weren't going to tip me anyway!"

By this time, Natty and I had had enough of these creepy clients. I announced to all the passengers: "Your ride is over. Get out!" They were in complete disbelief and refused to exit!

Mr. J wanted to fight me at this point. I told him I was going to call the police. Mrs. J said she was going to have us fired and that they'd be calling the owner. I happily told her that I wasn't merely the driver but this was my company!

I'm guessing she missed the fact that I was the owner even though my picture was on the side of the bus! What did she think? My photo was up there because I was the employee of the month? Natty and I got off and walked a safe distance away from the coach.

The Juice and his wife eventually exited the Ultra-Lounge and verbally threatened me. They said I'd never work in Orange County again! I laughed at them as we boarded the coach. I locked the door and drove past them, honking and flipping them off! We may not have gotten tipped but, in the end, we got back at them and it felt good! A true victory for the service industry, as so many of these types of people never get a dose of their own medicine!

> **NOTE:** *Ultra-Lounge was sold to a rock band from North Carolina and became their tour bus. They flew to California and drove it across the country, heading for the Carolinas. They broke down somewhere in Arkansas. I told them how to operate the bus but I could tell they weren't listening. They called me while I was in Miami on vacation. It was bad timing for them, as I was at a rooftop bar in South Beach. I never heard from them again. I'm not sure if they ever made it back to North Carolina.*

The Dream-Lounge

My business was picking up speed. The Hopper and Ultra-Lounge were booked regularly and people were enamored with the concept. There was still no competition; mine was the only RV limousine party bus available. It was time to grow the fleet again. With overwhelmingly positive responses to my motorhome conversions, I set out to find another coach. I took a drive over to Travel Land USA in Irvine, California. To my surprise, they were out of business. Disappointed, I drove back up the freeway and missed my exit. I was daydreaming about the new vehicle design and had inadvertently exited the freeway too soon. I ended up driving right past an RV dealership. I'll refer to it as "Mack Thompson's RV," to preserve anonymity.

I was checking out the coaches when a colorful salesman came up to me. He started with his razzle-dazzle approach to sales.

"What's your name?" I asked.

"I'm Wild Bill!"

"Really? Are you sure?"

He said, "Yep!"

With the same enthusiasm, I said, "Hi, my name is Captain Marky Mark!"

I liked my new name so much, I put it on my business cards. My passengers loved it! This was how I got my "aka."

Wild Bill and I climbed in and out of a few coaches. Then I saw the word "Dream" on the side of an RV parked in the middle of the lot. I went over to her. It was a Fleetwood American Dream motorhome. This was it! The name would stick. I'd found my dream bus! The deal was signed and I drove her home. The theme of this coach was obvious. I put an American Eagle slot machine onboard and made the interior snow-leopard-themed. A few months later, the conversion from RV to party bus was complete.

BAR MITZVAH PARTY BUST

One of my first trips on the Dream-Lounge was to a Jewish temple. My client had used my buses before and was making me a local on the bar mitzvah scene. She gave my number to everyone who needed a bar mitzvah. Funny thing was, while building these coaches, I never figured we'd be servicing Jewish temples.

I pulled up to the temple and parked. Apparently, it had tight security and the police were called. I was sitting in the cockpit when the officer tapped on my window and asked me to identify myself. I lowered the window and jokingly told him that my face was on the side of the bus! He wasn't laughing. In fact, his demeanor got meaner! When he asked me for a chauffeur's license, I knew he had no idea about the limousine business, its licensing requirements, etc.

I cautiously told him that there was no such license. That's when he said, "You need to exit the vehicle." I got out. He quickly put me up against the side of the coach and started the search! Just then, the kids and parents came out to witness their driver being interrogated at the curb by this overzealous lawman. My client intervened on my behalf and the officer allowed the passengers to board while mad-dogging me from his patrol car as I pulled off the curb. En route to drop off the kids, I noticed the cop was following the bus. I don't know what he even wanted in the first place! I got to the drop-off and there he was.

All the passengers exited the bus and the load door was still open. I was in the back, picking up all the yarmulkes left behind by the kids. I'd counted 30 of them and was thinking, *What am I going to do with all these tiny hats?* That's when the officer boarded the coach and found me. The interrogation continued! I gave him my commercial driver's license and registration.

He told me, "This bus was seen at a hotel and it was reported that the driver stole ice from one of their machines."

After a good laugh, I asked the officer if he could see any ice. These were young kids, and this was obviously not an adult party. They hired me for a pickup/drop-off and no drinks were onboard.

Not satisfied, the cop decided to search the vehicle. I figured this guy was rogue and I hoped he didn't plant anything. I followed him around the coach to make sure. He didn't like that and asked me to get off. I told him, "No, your search is over!" I explained that an RV is equal to a motor home. It qualifies as an actual second home, and one can get a mortgage on it. For a home, the police would need a search warrant. I also didn't consent to this search. Because I wasn't being placed under arrest and because I'd identified myself, I ordered him off the coach. To my surprise, he left. I put the coach in gear and got out of there! Unfortunately, this wouldn't be my last encounter with rogue lawmen.

NO COUPLES RETREAT

The Dream was booked one night by a company asking me to pick up its passengers in Newport Beach, with very short notice. I took the gig and went to the pickup. I had no information about the company or the event. I met the primary curbside in front of a restaurant and all the passengers got on board. They were scandalously dressed in all manner of adult attire. I introduced myself as The Captain. All the people were quiet and didn't seem to know each other. Puzzled, I closed the cockpit door and drove off. During my drive to L.A., I noticed that no music was coming from the back. Nobody was talking either. I found this to be odd. After all, this was a party bus, not a church bus, LOL!

I was asked to stop at a liquor store. While parked, I tried to chat up the passengers. Turned out, this was a singles cruise. The company was very discrete about its services. Nobody onboard knew each other. They were just a group of random horny adults. There were no online dating sites at that time.

The liquor was passed around and people started to mingle. I assumed their inhibitions were lowering when the whooping and hollering started.

A frantic knock on the cockpit door came from the primary renter, requesting that I pull off the freeway. I asked her what was going on. She explained that a couple was locked in the back room. This was an obvious design flaw on my part, as I should have removed the bedroom before renting out this bus. Because the bus used to be a motor home, I'd thought that the bedroom could be used to rest while waiting for customers to come out of their venues. However, I forgot to lock the passengers out of that room.

They were caught in the act! I knew I'd be burning the mattress and removing the bed after this gig! I had to use my key to get them out. They were still getting dressed as I opened the door! I gave them their clothes and let them out. This wouldn't be the last time I caught people fornicating on my bus. I'm not sure how many babies were conceived in my vehicles but at least they got a happy start! As for the rest of the passengers, I'm pretty sure they didn't get this lucky!

PROM BUS PARTY CRASHERS

Some teens from La Habra, California rented the Dream-Lounge for their high school dance in Long Beach, California. April, my new waitress, would be accompanying me as the chaperone. Her task was to make sure no minors were drinking. These types of reservations were often difficult, as I'd spend hours trying to track down parents. Getting the parents' signatures wasn't easy either. It always amazed me how they rarely got involved with these school dances unless something went horribly wrong. They were forced to get involved only after the kids got busted.

We picked up the teens and made it to their dance. The drop off was a traffic circle within the Long Beach Aquarium. There was room for me to park and off-load in front of a restaurant, leaving plenty of room for traffic to get around us.

Two cops watched me off-load the teens. They walked over toward the bus. They could see that I was busy but they threated to give me a ticket for parking there. I was thinking, *What is this guy's problem?* Both cops proceeded to give me a hard time in front of the teens, undermining my authority and embarrassing me. I told the teens that I'd be back in the same spot to pick them up. The cop yelled, "No, you won't!" The kids looked at me, confused, but I was out of time and had to move the coach before I got a ticket.

Later that night, I had to go back to pick up the teens. I was hoping the cops would have moved on by now. I parked at the curb and April prepared the cabin with waters for the kids. The teens started boarding. I did a final headcount. One couple was missing! I got off the bus and started looking for them. April was still in the back, tending to the kids and adjusting the stereo.

Through the window, I heard her yell for me! I ran back to the bus and saw two gang bangers onboard, terrorizing the teens. I asked them to leave but they wouldn't. I grabbed one and tried to throw him out the door. However, his hand caught the side of the door jamb and he managed to remain in the stairwell.

Then the same two cops walked up and again asked me to move the bus or be ticketed. I frantically told them that gang bangers had boarded and we needed help but they refused. Their only concern was that I move the bus.

I ran to the back of the coach, where I found the second banger, and chased him to the front door. They were both at the load door when April came flying in with a kick that knocked them out of the bus! I got off and started chasing them. This was all in front of the two cops, who remained there motionless! The bangers got away and I jogged back to the bus. I was in disbelief that the Long Beach Police Department had refused to help us. When we dropped off the passengers, they thanked us for saving them. They told us that it was a prom night they'd never forget! For all our efforts, neither April nor I received a tip or a thank-you call from any of the parents.

NOTE: Dream was my favorite bus and it was very hard to let her go. After she was sold, the new owner failed to pick her up. I stored Dream for three and a half months for him. I was able to squeeze in a few last runs, much to the delight of my regular clients. Finally, the day came when Dream left for Baltimore, Maryland. She is now servicing the East Coast. The new owner called me to confirm that he made it across the country. Though I no longer owned these buses, I was still concerned about them like a shepherd looking after lost sheeps.

The Mega-Lounge Double-Decker

PartyLounge Transportation was quickly gaining notoriety and growing expediently. My client base was outpacing the fleet and the capacity of the vehicles. So, I set out to find a new giant motor home for conversion. However, they simply didn't make RVs big enough to accommodate 30 or more passengers. My only option was to look for a big bus. The search was on for the "Mega-Lounge!"

Online, I came across an old for-sale post for a double-decker bus in Texas. I called the number and, much to my surprise, found that the coach was still available. However, four other companies were looking to purchase her. I quickly assembled a team consisting of a mechanic and a driver.

I casually told my wife that I'd be leaving the next day for a week to chase down a bus lead in Texas. She thought I was nuts! We'd miss each other because we were seldom apart but sometimes absence makes the heart grow fonder.

My team and I arrived at the airport and my mechanic got stopped by the TSA. He'd never flown before and had brought a big Buck Knife with him. I could see the TSA roughing him up a bit, so I walked back to security to see what was going on. He was a nice guy but acted like a redneck. I asked him why he'd brought the knife and he explained that it was his multipurpose tool. The TSA took away the knife and, surprisingly, let him go.

Getting to Dallas/Fort Worth, where Mega was housed, on such short notice was no easy task. The seller was flying in from Argentina. His name was Jose. We got settled in our room for the night with plans to meet Jose in the morning at his bus terminal. However, the next day, when we arrived at Hurricane Transportation, Jose was a no-show. I panicked because time is literally money, especially when you're footing the bill!

Jose showed up by late afternoon and we inspected the bus. Jose's mechanic tried to fire her up but it was apparent that the bus had been sitting in the weeds for years. I was extremely disappointed that we'd come all this way for what seemed like a big wild goose chase. Jose assured me he'd get the coach running by the next day. I was mad because the seller knew we were on a tight schedule. He should have had the bus ready for me.

The following day, we found the bus parked in the service bay. Jose's mechanic was still working on the coach. I pulled the mechanic aside and asked him when Mega would be roadworthy. He explained that it would take a few days.

I prepared my team for some R & R, as we were now playing the waiting game. We enjoyed several days of Dallas's finest bars, strip clubs, and restaurants before it was time to get serious again. It was costing me a fortune to hang out in Dallas with my team. However, I wasn't leaving without the Mega-Lounge. I gave Jose an ultimatum with a deadline. The bus miraculously got fixed and I paid him with a cashier's check for $156,000. I put my team on the road and flew home. Three days after I got back, the Mega-Lounge pulled into my bus terminal.

It was time to design a new vehicle for California's first true double-decker limousine bus. I started by pulling out all 60 seats. It was a huge task for one person but I managed. The coach was now empty on both levels. I installed a stereo system, speakers, monitors, a DVD player, and dance poles.

I drove the bus to the upholsterer, but it was too big to fit in the shop. The bus would have to be worked on in the parking lot. After a few days, I got a call. The bus had been broken into and all the electronics had been chopped. This was a huge setback in terms of time and money. Frustrated but not deterred, I repaired the damages.

Excited about the bus, I let it slip on social media that it would be coming soon and posted a photo. The calls came in and I had the first rental on the books. The date was approaching and I regretted my haste in taking reservations so soon.

The pressure was on, as I was running out of time to complete the bus conversion. The upholsterer was behind schedule and the bus still needed a paint job. She was yellow when I bought her and the team was calling her "The Big Banana"! The coach was going to be painted Limo Black.

Mega's size became an issue, as no paint booths were available for a two-story bus! After days of research, I finally found a company to do the job. Mega got her interior finished and the paint job was done with one day to spare before her first rental!

As it happened, I needed that extra day to fix the bathroom. The toilet worked on air and flushed like one you would find in an airplane. I'd never worked on a toilet like this. I found an obstruction in the drain line and I had to put together a crudely made scope and flashlight to see what it was. The initial search yielded a beer can that my redneck driver had accidentally dropped in there but was afraid to tell me about!

SHELL SHOCKED

The very first commercial driver I hired was a guy we'll call "M.S." (wink, wink!). M.S. is also an acronym for "Major Stupid"! M.S. was solid at first but then became complacent and lazy. He begged me to let him drive Mega. I eventually gave in. After training him on the operations of the bus, I gave him his first gig.

Mega was to pick up 60 teens and take them to their high school dance. The wife and I'd treated some friends to a quick trip to Hawaii to catch the Pro Bowl. We were at my favorite luau in Ko Olina, Oahu, called Paradise Cove. I was on my third Mai Tai and feeling great! I was wearing a grass skirt and playing Hawaiian games.

The staff invited me to join the performers and dance on stage. I took off my shirt and jumped on the stage. I busted out my former stripper moves and everyone thought it was hilarious!

As I was leaving the stage and receiving cheers, catcalls, and high-fives, my phone rang. This was trouble and I knew it! A frantic M.S. was on the other line, screaming, "I'm sorry, I'm so sorry!" etc. He'd just crashed the bus into a Shell station in Newport Beach. The passengers could be heard screaming in the background. I went from buzzed to sober in two seconds flat! How did this happen? M.S. explained that he was out of gas and had accidentally driven the bus into the canopy!

Ironically, one side of the station could have accommodated the coach. Instead, M.S. drove the Mega to the shorter side. Perplexed at his stupidity, and concerned and horrified at the same time, I asked, "How are the passengers? Is anybody hurt?" By the grace of God, there were no injuries. The teens called their parents and they all left the Shell station.

M.S. managed to cause $4,000 worth of damages to my bus and another $4,000 worth of damages to the Shell station. My small vacation was ruined. I had to fly home and fix everything. To make matters worse, there had been a mix-up with my room; my friends had gotten our penthouse suite while we had gotten their regular room. It's true what they say: "No good deed goes unpunished!"

FYI: M.S. was fired. No surprise there! To this day, I can't pass that station without thinking about the incident.

DRIVER ESCAPES

Mega-Lounge's next gig was also a memorable one. Freshly out of the shop from her maiden voyage, she was booked for yet another prom. Coincidentally, this dance was just down the street from where Mega had crashed a few weeks earlier. I was optimistic that all would go well but, just in case, I had one staff member on board to assist the driver.

I was driving the Dream-Lounge to the same dance when the call came in. My interior staff member said that Mega had crashed at the Hyatt in Newport Beach and that the driver was missing. I was already en route but pushed my bus hard to answer the emergency. When I got there, all chaos ensued! I found Mega at the bottom of a large hill that led to the lower parking lot. The bus was wrecked in the front and stuck on the hill because it couldn't traverse the steep angle of the hill as it descended to the lower parking lot. The coach was pinned at the bottom of the hill. Mega was stuck!

All the kids got off and walked to their dance, as it was on the property. I immediately found the steward who was chaperoning the gig. He explained that the Hyatt staff had insisted that the bus park in the lower parking lot and had directed our driver down the steep driveway.

My driver should have known that the coach was too long and too low to right itself at the bottom. He should have refused their commands. However, he didn't. In fact, he made matters worse, as I was about to find out.

I asked the steward, "Where's the driver?" He explained that the driver had excused himself to visit the restroom and had never come back. We started looking for him all over the Hyatt but it was obvious that he had left the scene of the accident. Just then, my wife called and said that the driver and his wife had pulled up to the house. The driver had hopped out and gotten into his car. Then they'd both driven off!

I asked the steward, "Where is the $3,200 the kids gave him?" We checked the onboard safe. The money was gone, too! I called the police to report the accident—now a robbery. While waiting for the Newport Beach Police to show up, I called a mobile mechanic. We needed him to assist in the rescue operation. I also called another driver, as we were now a driver short. The mechanic showed up and we removed the front bumper and headlamps. The bus couldn't go forward, so we tried to back it up the hill. However, the rear bumper was snagged by the steep angle of the driveway. With the bus in full reverse, I tried to push the front of it up the hill. Finally, the rear tire grabbed and pulled the coach backward. We got the bus back to the top of the hill and parked it.

I walked back down the hill, picked up a 150-pound bus bumper, and carried it back up the hill, to the amazement of the spectators. I gave the part to the mechanic and he started welding the brackets back on the bus. The Hyatt security came over and started hassling us. They wanted us to leave but any moron could look at the coach and know that it wasn't going anywhere.

I was already heated to the boiling point when the cops showed up. They proceeded to tell me that this was a domestic problem and refused to help. I explained to them that this was grand theft and they had to do something! I gave them the driver's address. They went over to his house, picked him up, and brought him back. He denied everything, of course! The cops let him go, stating I had no proof that he stole or did anything.

That was the snapping point for me. Just as I started arguing with the cops, I smelled something burning. I turned around to find that the mechanic had accidentally set the bus on fire! I grabbed the fire extinguisher and put it out. At this point, the cops were driving away. They refused to get involved or help. Other limo drivers ran over to console me. Then Hyatt security came back and started in on me again.

By this time, the kids from my bus and from Mega were out of their dance and standing near both coaches. Ninety kids watched the mechanic work while I argued with Hyatt security.

The mechanic finished repairing the bus just as my replacement driver showed up. He got into the Dream Bus and drove my group home. I stayed behind and drove Mega back to ensure everyone made it home safely.

The next day, I went after my stolen money but it wasn't to be, as the driver had left town and couldn't be found.

Throughout the years I've been hired to go back to the Hyatt Newport Beach but I've always made my staff drop off out front, on Jamboree Road. I'm always mindful to never send one of my buses onto that property again!

HUNTINGTON BEACH FOURTH OF JULY PARADE

I always wanted one of my buses to be in the Huntington Beach Fourth of July Parade. I'd requested this numerous times but was always denied by the parade committee. They ran it like an H.O.A. I knew a guy who was in it year after year with his scouts. One year, I asked him if he could get me in. He gave me a number to call and the meeting was set.

The parade board came to my bus terminal and looked at my buses. They chose the Mega-Lounge double-decker. I was told it would be perfect as the "Freedom Bus." The theme of the parade was "Waves of Freedom." The parade entry fee was $1,200 but they claimed I'd make the money back with the television coverage.

I thought that cutting a check and showing up was all I had to do. Not even close! A week later, I received an email with a list of their demands. They wanted me to remove all my corporate logos, my phone numbers, my web address, etc. I was then told how they wanted the bus decorated. I was also asked to uninstall all the bottom windows so that the crowd could see the World War II vets. This was no easy task, as you can't drive a bus with no windows on the highway. So, I had to design them to be removed in the field before the bus entered the parade route. They also wanted a marching banner. It was to be held and walked in front of the bus. The board's list of demands was getting ridiculous!

I wanted to make changes of my own. I made the top-deck windows open like Gull Wings. I figured the crowd might as well see me, too!

The big day came and I parked on Pacific Coast Highway, then started getting the bus ready. I was just removing the lower windows when the fire marshal walked up and asked to see my fire extinguisher. I showed him where it was. He said it was out of date! I argued that it was only by a few months. However, he would make no exceptions! I told him the needle was still indicating it was good but he wouldn't allow the bus to be in the parade unless we replaced it with a new one.

Time was ticking. I had to run from house to house, knocking on doors, asking anyone if they had a current extinguisher. The fire marshal was being difficult.

A friend was passing by and saw my bus. She walked up and I asked her for help. She came through and got a fire extinguisher for me minutes before the parade started. I let her ride on Mega in the parade. I almost went through all that time, expense, and effort to be sidelined by an out-of-date fire extinguisher.

As we traveled up the parade route, I could see the TV cameras. I thought we were going to be interviewed because the bus looked so amazing! Mega had all her Gull Wing windows opened to the sky, while the lower ones were off completely. You could see all the World War II vets, who were all in their 90s. To my disbelief, the cameras cut away to some F'N Whiskey Tango that was on foot and talking about figs! I called my wife, who was watching from home, and she confirmed that we were on the air for only a few seconds. Why would the network not want to show the Freedom Bus with the last Tuskegee Airman and World War II vets onboard? I was so pissed off and disappointed.

PartyLounge didn't receive any leads as a result of being in that parade!

The next year, the parade committee called me up and wanted me to do it all over again. I never got back to them!

NOTE: *The Mega-Lounge was another one of my favorite buses. She was the fastest bus to sell. I could have sold her ten times over. Companies and even* private parties wanted to buy her. She was a rare bus, indeed. The new owner is a very nice guy and we're still in contact. He has taken extremely good care of her and even made some of his own modifications. The bus has been on the local news in Ohio and in the paper. He has plans to make a TV show about her. I wish him luck! Best wishes, Team Johnson! I'm available for a cameo walk-on role.

The Land Yacht

By far, the most incredible bus I've ever owned was the Land Yacht. This bus was a Prevost H560. Only 46 of them were ever built. I felt honored to be one of the very few owners, and most likely the only private owner outside of a big corporation.

It was a 60-foot articulating five-axle city liner touring coach. This bus was tall and looked like a double-decker bend bus. The bottom level was for cargo and the top floor was for passengers. It originally had seats for 71 passengers but I converted it into an 80-passenger by redesigning the interior.

The Land Yacht was by far the most expensive bus I've ever owned and operated. It would be the sister bus to the majorly successful Mega-Lounge.

I started looking for her but she'd be a rare find. I recalled seeing a coach that looked like Mega in Dallas, Texas. I called Jose from Hurricane Transportation. He confirmed that he had the bus. It was virtually the same as the Mega-Lounge, only it wasn't a double-decker.

I figured this would be fine because both buses looked the same. So, I put together my team and we flew out to see it. Jose was a no-show again but this time I didn't wait for him. My driver, mechanic, and I drove to Hurricane Transportation's bus terminal and saw the coach sitting in the tall weeds.

I had a bad feeling that this most likely was a fool's errand. However, being hopefully optimistic, we walked around the bus.

She was in bad shape, with a cracked windshield, flat tires, and the driver's door strapped down, to list just a few visuals. I forced my way inside to find the interior covered in dust and cobwebs.

I liked the floor plan but this bus was a filthy mess. Trash, rat droppings, feathers, and the weather had all made their way inside the coach through the broken roof hatches. It was obvious the owners weren't maintaining the vehicle. We tried to start it but the batteries were dead.

Jose knew we were coming all the way from California again; why wouldn't he have this coach ready? The staff at Hurricane Transportation told me to come back the next day and they'd have it running.

Not wanting to waste any more time, money, or effort on this bus, I contemplated leaving. However, because we were in town and had come this far, I made the executive decision to give them a few days. The next morning, I showed up to micro-manage them into getting us on the road.

Jose still hadn't shown up. It turned out he was still in Argentina! Their mechanic was very nice and honest. He felt bad for me and tried hard to get the big bus running. I stayed in contact with him. On the third day, the bus was still not road-worthy.

I went back to my hotel to think about my next move. Then their mechanic called me. He said that Jose had shown up and wouldn't authorize any of the necessary repairs. He wanted me to pay for the work. In addition, the repairs would take two weeks to complete.

I was so upset by the news that we immediately packed up our gear and flew home to Los Angeles. Jose tried to talk me into coming back to Dallas. This guy was a real piece of work. I told him off and hung up on him!

Back at my home office, I continued the search. I made many calls and put the feelers out. A week after I got back from Dallas, a lead came in. I received a call from a big bus company in Los Alamitos, California. They told me about a guy in Montebello who was selling a giant bus and gave me his number. I called the guy, who confirmed that he had a very large bus and that it could hold 71 people.

I drove up to see her. I'll never forget the moment. I walked around the coach and thought, *My God, this is the biggest bus I've ever seen! It's like a yacht on land.* That's how she got her name, the Land Yacht.

The bus was idling when I got there and everything checked out with my mechanic. I bought her and drove back to my bus terminal in Huntington Beach. I was so excited to get started on the bus conversion. I had 71 seats to remove. I got that done in one day! We started building the limousine-style parameter seating and then took the bus to the upholsterer. Because the bus was too big to hide, people started coming by my bus terminal to see it. It was getting lots of interest and it could have been booked before I turned it into a limo. However, a job of this magnitude couldn't be rushed, so we declined the business until I could be sure she was ready.

The stereo system, lighting, and other electrical applications proved to be very difficult, as the wiring had to run through the bend joint in the center of the bus. If we didn't give the wires enough slack, they'd break when the bus made a turn. My engineering skills were put to the test on this build-out.

We had to drive around, making turns to see which speaker got disconnected. Then we'd length the wires as necessary. Too many wires meant they'd interfere with other components placed there by the original manufacturer.

It was amazing to open the turn stall platform where the bus bent. Lots of parts were stuffed in there. Toward the back of the coach, I installed a bar. I also had to repair everything in the bathroom. The last thing to be done was to have the bus wrapped black with blue flames. This would be cheaper and faster than painting. She looked insane and was a real head-turner as we went down the highway!

THE INSPECTOR

Registering this bus was a challenge. Any bus coming into the California Department of Motor Vehicles must be seen by a DMV inspector. To bring a 60-foot bus into the small DMV parking lot wasn't possible. I had to park it at the curb along the adjoining street.

I went inside and asked them to send out their guy. I waited over an hour but nobody came outside. I went back into the DMV and they rudely stated that if I wanted my bus to be inspected, I had to drive it around the building to the inspection area. I tried to explain the laws of physics to these imbeciles but they weren't getting it.

I went back outside to take a picture of the bus, then showed it to them. "Now do you understand that this coach will not fit in your inspection area?" I asked.

At this point, they sent their inspector, "Gilbert," outside to the parking lot. He took one look at the bus and said, "Where's the engine located?"

My first thoughts were, *Aren't you the inspector, and why am I here?* I walked Gilbert over to the engine compartment.

He looked at it and then asked, "Where's the other engine?"

I thought, *You've got to be kidding me!* However, Gilbert wasn't kidding. I explained to him that all buses have only one engine!

Gilbert went back into the DMV and got a colleague. Both looked over the bus, bewildered looks on their faces.

Gilbert stated to me, "It's too long to be on the road. You're not going to be able to register it."

I informed him that because it bent in the middle, it could be legally registered as a commercial vehicle. The banter went back and forth but it was a losing battle. They simply wanted nothing to do with me or my bus. It was obvious that they wanted to get rid of me so they could go back to inspecting small cars.

I drove the Land Yacht to another DMV. This time, success! The inspector just glanced at the bus, took down the VIN number, and signed off on the paperwork. It just goes to show you how lazy some people are. The first DMV was a nightmare to deal with.

THE CALABASAS CLAN

One of the Land Yacht's first gigs was in the lavish city of Calabasas, where some of the elite Hollywood entertainers and producers live. The client was a cougar with an attitude; we'll call her "Candy." You know I can't tell you her real name. Candy was sour like some confections, so don't let the name fool you! She was anything but sweet!

She phoned me and the short conversation was the first red flag! I knew this lady was going to be trouble from start to finish. However, I had so much money invested in this coach, I had to get her out on the road.

Despite my better judgment, I rented to Candy. The bus arrived at her multi-million-dollar gated community but nobody was in sight. Although my contract and our conversation stated that the bus couldn't pick up at her house, she refused to have the teens outside of the community, as we had planned. I was forced to go into the gated community and get them. I'm sure this was her plan all along.

I pulled up to the tiny guard gate. To do it, I used both the visitor lane and the homeowner lane. The guard came out, as residents were honking behind me, trying to get in. The gate opened and there was no going back! Cars were on my tail, so the rear of the coach had to clear trees, walls, street lamps, etc. As I nosed it forward, it became apparent that I was going to have to back up and scissor the coach in. I had to put the bus in "park," walk to the rear, and ask everyone to back up and give me room. To make matters worse, they all had an attitude. I was in no mood to take any of their nonsense.

I went back to the cockpit and just started to reverse. I figured if they saw the bus rolling back, they'd get out of the way!

After getting through the first obstacle (the front gate), I came to a giant hill. Of course, this was her street! The bus slowly made its way up as the people from the front gate went flying around me, honking and flipping me off! I was almost at the top when the coach overheated and the "check engine" light came on. This automatically shut down the engine. The bus put itself into "safe mode!" Panicked and not sure what to do, I got on the phone and called the former owner. Luckily for me, he answered. He was telling me how to get the engine temperature down when I got an incoming call from the client. She was mad because I hadn't arrived yet.

To add to all my frustration and confusion, a parent had driven by and seen me parked. She came over to see the bus, which was the last thing I needed. I didn't want to tell them it was dead in the water. I was afraid to restart it and I was waiting for it to cool down. So, I had to pacify her by stating that I'd pulled over to use the restroom in the bus and that I'd be up the hill in a minute. Thank God it worked! She drove off but, unfortunately, told Candy that I was parked nearby.

Candy called and ordered me to get to her place or else. I kept thinking to myself, *If the bus won't start, I'm going to lose $4,000 and be stuck in this gated community with no rescue for me or the kids.* I said a quick prayer and tried the key. The bus engine roared to life but was still hot. I followed the directions given to me by the former owner and engaged the bus's high idle, which brought down the temperature. I put the bus in gear and started climbing the hill again. As I was about to crest the hill, the bus didn't have enough power to go forward. I was so close! I downshifted the coach into the lowest gear and we finally made it. I pulled up in front of Candy's multi-million-dollar estate. The bus was smoking.

Eighty teens were out front to witness my arrival. Relieved that I'd finally made it, I got out of the driver's chair and regained my composure. I opened the load door and introduced myself as Captain Marky Mark. The teens loved it and I continued to put on an act for them. I was in character and wanted to win them over so they'd cooperate with me throughout the night.

I had suggested to the primary that she have a chaperone on board because there were so many kids. When I met her, the first thing she asked was, "Where's the chaperone?" I told her that if I'd brought my own people to chaperone, the liability would be on me. I reminded her that our rental contract stated that it was up to the renters to provide a chaperone. At this point, I figured she was too cheap to pay for one and I could expect no tip from her.

I tried to win her over with kindness and diplomacy but she was rude and condescending, belittling me and my company, as well as undermining my authority in front of the kids. Knowing that nothing I did or said could make this lady happy, I began to load the kids as fast as I could! Pulling off the curb, I could see Candy glaring at me. It's hard to believe someone that attractive could act so ugly.

I drove to the kids' prom, and the principal was there waiting. He and a select group of personnel were off-loading the kids and inspecting the interior of the bus. They were doing their booze inspection. Five minutes into the search, they found some! The principal came to me and wanted to hold me responsible for contributing to the delinquency of minors. He also called the police, making a huge deal out of it. One of the kids was, indeed, intoxicated. I explained our contract to him. Our protocol was to call the primary renter; it was up to her to inform all the kids' parents.

We had no authority to search their belongings. Because the principal had opened the girl's purse to get the liquor, he was out of his jurisdiction, too. I assured him I'd be pointing this out to the cops when they showed up. The police arrived and interrogated me and all the kids. They boarded the Land Yacht and continued to search. They found more liquor. This gig was an absolute shit show!

I showed the police the signed rental contract between Candy and me. I explained to him that the primary was to have a chaperone. Satisfied that I wasn't involved or responsible, he agreed. I drove off without the kids.

Once I was a few miles from the dance, I pulled over to make the dreaded phone call to Candy. She had a nasty disposition, so I knew this wasn't going to be good news. She answered the phone and I explained what had happened.

She said, "Of course you're going to have to go pick them up!"

I referred her to our contract, pointing out the provision that read, "If alcohol is found while minors are present, the ride is terminated on the spot."

Candy yelled, "I'm going to sue you!" She reminded me that her husband was a high-powered entertainment lawyer.

By this time, I had no patience left and said, "Bring it on! Have fun picking up your drunk kids!"

The next week, her husband called, threatening me and wanting me to return the $4,000. I told him that, as per our rental contract, I offered no refunds to people who committed crimes on my bus. He tried to intimidate me but I held my ground! He threatened to sue me for the $4,000 plus damages and wanted me to refund all 80 kids for their expenses. I told him that he was a bad example of parenting and to assign blame, they needed to look no further than themselves. He knew he had no case because his signature was on the contract. Also, I'd had all the kids sign a separate contract called the "Leslie Bill" to ensure they wouldn't drink on my bus.

Apparently, in their world, they can all act the fool at others' expense! Maybe it's because they're so darn special! I told Lawyer Blowhard that I'd already spoken to the principal and could supply him with a list of everyone on board the bus. Being that this was a school-sanctioned function, the principal told me the school had the authority to punish their kids with suspension or expulsion!

I also told Attorney Blowhard not to persist or I'd make sure the principal got that list of kids! I never heard back from him. This may be one case he lost before it even got started! I was certain he was pissed, and his ego was tarnished at having lost a case to a bus driver. He had the kids write my company bad Yelp reviews—none of which had any merit or truth. Yelp saw through most of these posts and deleted all but one of them. In the end, the Land Yacht and I'd live again to face more moronic people.

NASTY CORP

The Land Yacht's next assignment was for a corporation in Orange County. The primary had a personal assistant, and I was working with her. It made things difficult because everything I told her had to be relayed to her boss. I could see things were getting lost in translation.

They booked the Land Yacht for their corporate Christmas party. The pickup would be at their office and then we'd head to a charter boat in Newport Beach. Their harbor booze cruise would last three hours.

I picked up all 55 passengers on time and got on the road. It was always important to arrive early when passengers were trying to make it to a boat. They were pleased that I arrived extra early and they used the time to pick up liquor.

The Land Yacht isn't the best vehicle in which to run errands. They should have bought booze beforehand. However, I agreed to take them. I located a liquor store on Pacific Coast Highway. I pulled over and turned on my hazard lights. I explained to the primary that we were on borrowed time, as there is no parking on PCH and certainly not for a 60-foot bus. I was also concerned about getting them to their boat on time. They assured me they'd be quick.

Ten minutes went by and nobody had come out of the store. I watched the clock nervously, as they were going to expect me to race this big coach to the dock. Fifteen minutes went by and I called them. It turned out that these morons were smoking and drinking in the parking lot adjacent to the store. I yelled at them to get on the bus. As they were walking over, a cop pulled up and detained them for drinking in public.

This was supposed to be an easy job—just pick them up and drop them off. However, there's no such thing as an easy gig when alcohol is involved! I pleaded with the cop to just give them a warning, explaining to him that we were leaving. He also wanted my bus out of there. He decided to let us leave without a ticket or arresting anyone. He probably figured it would be too much paperwork or hassle for such minor offenses.

Back on board, I was the hero for having gotten them out of trouble. However, our time was running out. I started up the Land Yacht and blasted down the highway. I had to make a U-turn in that big bus, which was no easy task. I pulled off the maneuver and floored it down the highway. Just as we were making great strides, a Prius pulled in front of the bus, forcing me to slam on the brakes and miss the signal. I was honking and throwing a fit, and I'm sure the passengers could hear me cursing!

Arriving dockside, I offloaded everyone in time for their event. Relieved that this portion of the night was over, I found a place to park so I could get some rest. A neighbor saw the bus parked on her street. She came up to the load door and started knocking. I asked her what she wanted and the lady went off on me. I told her to relax but that made things worse. She was one of those snotty, entitled, pain-in-the-butt types and was offended that my bus was parked across the street from her house. She complained that it was an eyesore, too loud, and smelly. I explained the bus was going to be parked there for only a few hours and would be shut off. Nevertheless, she threatened to call the cops on me if I didn't leave. I told her to go ahead and then went to the back of my bus to lie down.

A patrol car pulled up. It was the same cop I'd dealt with at the liquor store. He said, "It's you again! What is it going to take to get you and this big bus out of my town?"

I told him why I was there but this time, he wasn't having any of it. To make matters worse, the homeowner came out to put in her two cents. I started to lose my composure and yelled back at her. The cop saw what a complete bitch this lady was and told me to just take off. That's what I did.

I found a school not too far away and parked. Just as I was getting in some much-needed rest, the primary called. The boat had taken them back to the dock early because their group was too intoxicated. From that call, I knew that the trip back was going to be trouble.

I showed up at the dock and told everyone to get on, as I was blocking a lane on Pacific Coast Highway to pick them up. They all just stood there, smoking and stumbling around. I managed to round up half of them like a shepherd after drunk sheep! Some people walking by thought it was funny and started filming us. Then some of the girls started flashing their boobs to oncoming traffic. I was trying frantically to get them all on board when the police showed up.

"Good grief, what is going on here? I thought I told you to leave town!"

I responded, "I'm trying, Officer, but I could sure use your help in getting all these people on board."

Seeing that I was in over my head at this point and completely outnumbered by drunks, the policeman helped me get them on the Land Yacht. The cop turned to me and said, "This had better be the last I see of you and this bus tonight!"

I told him, "Nothing personal but you've got it!"

Traveling back to their office, I could hear people acting nuts in the back but no way was I pulling over. I got them back to their office and parked. When the passenger door opened, a river of spilled liquor came rushing down the aisle and onto the steps. The people spilled out of that bus like wet noodles on a slide. The mess they'd made was substantial! I was thinking this night couldn't be any worse when some chick fell into my arms as she tripped out the door. Holding her up and realizing that she had just puked on herself, I gently set her down on the sidewalk.

I managed to get them all out and close the load door. I was just about to make my escape when two of the drunk passengers stepped right in front of the bus and I almost ran them over. I got out of the bus and pushed them out of the way. They were drunk and said I wouldn't be getting a tip.

I told them, "I'm giving you a tip; never call me again!"

As I got back to my bus terminal and pulled in, the primary called and said she'd left her purse onboard. She told me that I had to come back and drop it off.

I told her, "Well, now, it seems to me that I got no tip and my bus is a disaster inside. So, I respectfully decline!"

She started yelling through the phone and I hung up on her. Then I texted her that she could get her purse in the morning. The next day, she still wanted me to bring her the purse. I told her I wasn't operating a lost-and-found or delivery service. She drove to my bus terminal where I was cleaning the bus. When she got there, I handed her the purse and watched her drive away. Not once did she thank me for anything or apologize. It's hard for me to believe that people can act this poorly. It just goes to show that having money and a position of power at your job does not give you class.

NOTE: *The Land Yacht was bought by a multi-millionaire from Bakersfield, California. He needed her to transport his employees. He had his own airplane and flew down to Santa Ana Airport, where I picked up him and his team. I was so sad to see her leave my bus terminal for the last time that I filmed her exit. This bus video has received more than one million views on YouTube.*

The Future Lounge

After much success with the big buses, Mega-Lounge and the Land Yacht, I decided to get a bus that was intermediate in size—not too big and not too small. I needed a 48-passenger coach. I'd always wanted to do a science-fiction-themed bus. I searched locally in Southern California for a coach that was art deco in design. My search led me to Los Angeles, where I found a late-model TMC, or Travel Management Company, bus. This coach was exactly the platform I was looking for. These vehicles are often used in movies and TV shows. They're also known as RTS, or Rapid Transit Series, buses. I struck a deal with the owner and was soon on the road to my bus terminal.

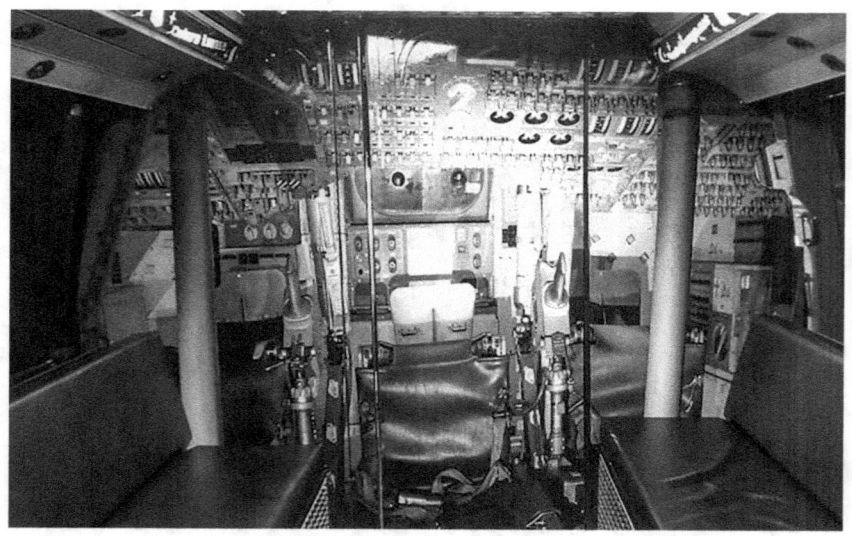

The key to building a bus is to find a chassis that has been in production for a while; that way, you can find parts. This bus was solid and a workhorse. I quickly transformed her into the Future Lounge. She had a bar, two stripper poles, a bathroom, two load doors, and a sci-fi-themed bulkhead divider, interior, and exterior wrap. People loved her. The bus was booked on a regular basis.

THE PLUS SIZE CHA CHAS

A phone call came from a woman frantic for a bus, which she needed within a few hours. I answered the phone while my wife and I were at dinner in our favorite restaurant, located at the top of Mandalay Bay in Las Vegas. Wifey got mad at me for answering the phone. I told her if she liked eating there, I was going to have to take the call. Leaving her at the table with a glass of her favorite champagne, I was able to take the booking from the patio. My thoughts were that Wifey would get over it and we could have a good time while making money.

However, the client turned out to be a huge pain in the ass. She was one of those extremely needy types and it all blew up in my face. The girl wouldn't stop calling me all through dinner. She had my driver completely frustrated, and now he was calling and texting me too. My wife was getting madder and madder at the constant interruptions. I ended up heading back to our hotel room to quarterback the gig. Upon getting to my room, I set up my laptop computer and tracked the bus. To my surprise, it hadn't left the pickup address yet. I learned from the driver that the primary was waiting for her friends and didn't want to pay for the downtime. She felt that my company should automatically eat the clock. She got irate when my driver tried to explain to her that that wasn't what the contract said.

The primary's hometown was Pico Rivera, California, and it wasn't the safest neighborhood to be in. It was a known gang-banger neighborhood. My driver felt uncomfortable and wanted to get the Cha-Chas loaded and on the road.

The gig was a bachelorette party and a poorly planned one at that. The primary and her friends finally boarded the bus. The driver noticed that they were all dressed like hookers, all stuffed into tiny apparel.

It was obvious they wanted attention. They instantly started complaining about everything. My driver tried to make them happy but the Cha-Chas remained difficult to deal with. Bad attitudes mixed with liquor earned them their names. They were all making this weird noise as they spoke their broken English; my driver said it sounded like a train coming. So, he named them the Cha-Chas!

Halfway to L.A., they ran out of toilet paper. They'd managed to go through two full rolls. They also ran out of liquor and ice, and somehow this was our fault as a company. We finally got them to the club in L.A. and they complained that there wasn't enough room on the bus.

The next day, they called me demanding a refund because they didn't all get a seat. Some of them had to stand. I told them occupancy wasn't guaranteed due to individual size, which I couldn't foresee from a phone call. This was also on the contract they signed! They made such a BIG deal out of it, pun intended! They were trying to get a free ride, discount, or refund out of me.

I asked my driver just how big the Cha-Chas were. He responded politely that they took up two times the space of a normal person and bent the dance pole! Considering this information, the primary didn't receive any compensation or discounts.

I charged her for the bent dance pole. She was mad, of course. She took to Yelp to complain about our services, as if we were to blame for her group's obesity and aggression toward stripper poles!

Commentary: "I don't need clients who think that society owes them a favor." These big bitches were rude, cheap, and classless. Yet, they expected preferential treatment. They didn't even tip my driver after all they put us through.

I have a tip for them: "Call another company next time!"

DRIVING MS. CRAZY

We scheduled the Future Lounge for a Hollywood run. These are often very difficult because people get drunk in the club and spill out into the street, making the pickup very problematic. The lack of parking, the traffic, and the pedestrians add to the equation.

The client, "Chiquita," was a whiny, narcissistic, entitled little "B"! I had the extreme displeasure of having her reservation on my calendar.

My new driver, "Pauly," was taking more gigs for the experience. I was grooming him to be the full-time operator of Future Lounge. Pauly picked up Chiquita and her crew of miscreants, who had already been drinking at their house. Almost immediately, she complained about the bus. She didn't bring her own music and thought we should have supplied it. Most people had music on their phones, and we provided the auxiliary cord. All this information was in our rental agreement. However, most people sign without bothering to read it.

Shortly thereafter, she complained that the air-conditioning was too cold. Then she complained that the bar had no stools.

Eventually, Pauly was so discombobulated from all her demands that he lost track of time and direction. Whenever she needed something, he would have to pull over and address the issue.

Future Lounge finally pulled into Hollywood but it was after the free-entry time at the club. Of course, the primary blamed our driver for making them late. She expected him to pay the cover charge for their entire party!

Pauly managed to get them off the coach and started hunting for a parking spot. He informed me about what had transpired and warned me to expect a call.

Chiquita called me to blame everything on us and wanted a full refund. That's when I decided to refund half the part—the part where we take them home!

I called Pauly and told him to bring back the bus. I surmised that Chiquita hadn't read the contract. I pointed out to her that we could terminate the rental at any time. She was shocked at my course of action.

Nevertheless, I wouldn't allow my employees or me to be disrespected. I also knew her behavior would be even worse on the ride back. Chiquita and her drunken crew of reprobates were left in Hollywood, where they had to hire another company to deal with them. I sure feel sorry for whoever picked them up!

PARTY PATROL

Future Lounge was deployed to our local highway patrol with my best driver, Hoss. I sent him there to get a special endorsement on his license, called a SPAB, or Student Pupil Activity Bus. Only the highway patrol can issue this and one must take a driving test with them to pass. So, Hoss pulled into the CHP, California Highway Patrol, for his appointment.

The officer that day was Nasty Toilette. Of course, this isn't her real name, as I couldn't possibly tell it to you. However, I'd sure like to!

Hoss is a big, friendly guy with a heart of gold. Nasty immediately started in on him as if he'd committed a crime. Then she started to inspect the Future Lounge and pick it apart. Not only was she not going to allow Hoss to drive for his test but she wanted to red-tag the bus! She threatened to impound Future Lounge over ridiculous things!

Hoss was very upset and worried when he placed a frantic call to me. He put Nasty on the phone. She began to tell me that she was confiscating the bus. I asked her why and explained to her that the bus had already passed an annual CHP inspection!

She was concerned that our license plate lamp was burned out, as were a few interior lights. This wasn't enough to place a bus out of service, so I demanded that she release my bus and driver immediately!

I contacted one of my clients, who worked out of that office. He was able to convince her to let us go.

A few weeks later, the same highway patrolman booked the Future Lounge. He needed it for a concert at Dodger Stadium in Los Angeles. He asked me to pick up his group at the same highway patrol office where Nasty worked. Fearful that we'd run into her, I mentioned the incident. He assured me that there would be no problems.

The booking date came and I sent Hoss to pick them up. He worried about going back to that CHP office. When he arrived to pick up the group of highway patrol officers, the first person out to receive him was Nasty!

She looked at my driver, then at the bus, and walked over. Luckily, she wasn't going to be a passenger. However, she did check to see if I'd replaced the burnt-out lights. I most certainly had but she started to nitpick other things on the bus. The primary renter walked out of the CHP and came to our defense.

Wow, we'd never seen patrol officers go at each other like that. Apparently, she wasn't very well-liked among her colleagues. Perhaps that's why they didn't invite her.

We got on the road and left Nasty back at the station. However, our days of dealing with her weren't over. Thankfully, a year later, I learned that she'd been sent to a different department. We'd never have to deal with her again!

At Dodger Stadium, a patrolman started tailgating. Some L.A. County sheriffs walked up to the patrol officers, who weren't in uniform, telling them that there was no parking in the parking lot. The sheriffs ordered the officers back on the bus and told them they had to either leave or go directly into the concert. The patrol officers pulled out their badges and identified themselves as CHP.

Heated arguments started between the two groups. It was the second time we'd witnessed lawman against lawman on the same day. Way too much testosterone on display here!

The CHP yelled, "You can't tell us what to do!"

The sheriffs yelled back, "Yes, we can!"

Hoss stepped into the middle and was able to defuse the standoff by offering the sheriffs a discount on their ride if they booked with us. He also offered the CHP extra time on the coach for the ride home. The CHP accepted and left the bus peacefully.

When the concert was over, one passenger was missing. He never made it back to the bus. When Hoss asked the primary renter why they were leaving without him, he explained that his friend had gotten so drunk that he'd gone into the band's "green room." This was where they got dressed and hung out before the concert. He then puked all over the lead singer's wardrobe and passed out.

Sure wish I could tell you the name of that singer. Here's a hint: His first name rhymes with "toy" and his last name with "forage." Get it? Good luck!

NOTE: *The Future Lounge had a sad ending. The buyer and his son flew down from Minnesota, where they were going to start a party bus company. The dad was a retired school bus driver and was going to drive the bus all the way back. Because he and his son had no experience operating a party bus, I took the time to teach them the workings of the coach. I also took them on a test drive but I had a bad feeling about the situation. When I gave them directions back to Minnesota, I specifically told them NOT to cross the Colorado Rockies but to go around and drive through the flat states.*

When they set off, I tracked them with my GPS app. They reached Vail, Colorado, and there the bus stopped. Future Lounge started sending me a signal for help. They continued traveling for a month. Eventually, all four of her batteries died. My theory was that they blew the head gasket. They most likely overheated the engine by driving through the Rockies. I believe they abandoned the bus. To this day, I have no idea where she is.

The Party Train

The Party Train is a 1999 Neoplan AN460 articulation bus, commonly referred to as a "bend bus."

After the huge success of Mega-Lounge and the Land Yacht, calls came in from all over Southern California for the big coaches. My business had found a niche.

The crowds started getting larger. I did some research and found that one of these buses could carry 100 passengers, so I set out to locate one for PartyLounge.

Typically, these are city buses. With any luck, I could persuade them to sell me one. I put out my feelers and struck gold in Houston, Texas.

The Houston Metropolitan Transportation Authority was getting ready to put its diesel fleet on the market. It was making room for its new CNG (Compressed Natural Gas) buses. I'd have been happy to have had one of their old diesel buses. I sent a team out to Houston to look them over. I liked the design of the coach so much that I made a deal for two of them. The Party Train and the Land Yacht 2.0 were heading to their new home: the PartyLounge bus terminal. This would be my final purchase, as I capped off my fleet at eight buses. This was a lot of equipment to maintain and store. Storage had always been a problem and we often had to change locations. Finding good mechanics had always been an issue, too!

THE STORAGE YARD FOR VERMIN

My fleet was parked in a commercial lot in the city of Costa Mesa, California. It was a small parking lot, and we were outgrowing the location. It was very expensive and had a high crime rate. There was also an old guy who was a problem neighbor. He owned a laundromat next to my lot and every time we started a bus, he would complain. The guy was a real jerk! On occasion, he would purposely block our gate. I'd have to continually ask him to move his car.

Nighttime was no better, as homeless drug addicts would loiter in front of our gate. Concerned about myself and my staff, I searched for a new bus terminal.

After weeks of looking for a new location, I found a facility. Drydock Storage was in a better part of Costa Mesa and appeared to be an upgrade.

I gathered up all my drivers and we moved the fleet. It was cool to see all our buses on the road, caravanning like a party parade! I remember traffic honking and people staring at us. This was also a great way to advertise, and it generated a few calls. So, once a month, we'd all hit the road together to generate leads through direct marketing. This proved to be a very effective way to advertise!

Drydock was located between two freeways. A few other limousine companies were parked there. After a few months, we learned that they weren't thrilled about having us as fellow tenants.

Drydock had a wash rack, which was always monopolized by the same limo company. I rarely got to use it and had to have a mobile service come out to wash our buses. They also had a dumpsite, which was frequently blocked by people washing their cars. I tried to make the best of the situation because no other local facilities were capable of housing PartyLounge.

An illegal moving company operated out of Drydock. One day, while I was on vacation, an employee of Drydock called to notify me that my bus had been in an accident.

I said, "How is that possible? The coach is currently parked."

It turned out, their security footage showed that the moving company had backed into one of my buses, shoving the load door into the interior of the coach. Then they took off and tried to hide the evidence.

I had to confront these dirtbags. They denied the whole event. I made them aware of the video footage and they finally fessed up. I tried to file a police report but the cops couldn't care less about the damage and never did anything to the moving company. The damages cost me over $2,000 to repair. I tried to collect from the moving company but it moved out of Drydock in the middle of the night.

A few months later, Party Train's fuel was stolen. I couldn't believe it. This place had fuel thieves, too! I figured it was an inside job. A few weeks later, the Mega-Lounge's fuel was also stolen. We set up a sting operation and found that it was the same dirtbags from the moving company. They still had an active code for the storage yard because the management had never deactivated it. They were visiting at night and breaking into vehicles. They eventually got caught. I'm not sure what the outcome was.

A few months later, we started having mechanical problems with the buses—strange things like blinkers not working, damaged taillights and headlights, etc. I was finding chewed wires. It was obvious that there was a vermin infestation at Drydock.

I went to the management to plead with them to remedy the situation, as I was spending hundreds of dollars in repairs because of the rodents. The management denied having any such problem and refused to act. They made it clear that they wouldn't be responsible for the damages.

I started putting out poison and managed to kill a few of them. I also trapped one and brought it alive to the front office to prove to them that they had rats. The lady at the front desk screamed when I brought in the rat! It was so funny and I got my point across.

Unfortunately, the rat problem grew out of control. It was costing me thousands in damages. Drydock got tired of me complaining about the problem and evicted PartyLounge. I was in disbelief at the thought of a company that would rather lose its highest-paying tenant than take care of a problem.

I contacted a lifelong friend who works in commercial real estate. He found me a vacant lot in Santa Ana. The PartyLounge fleet was on the move again.

I wrote Drydock a scathing review on Yelp. A year later, they went out of business!

THE MECHANIC FROM HELL

My mechanic was expensive, always booked, and unreliable, so I started using Cary's Mobile Mechanic. Although I noticed small problems with my buses, I gave them an opportunity to make things right. The buses continued to break down. I took them to another mechanic for a second opinion, and he verified that my fleet was being sabotaged. Cary's mechanic was creating more work for himself by installing inferior or used parts. We even found parts on the bus that were spray-painted to look new!

The first sign of trouble was that the transmission was a rebuild, though we paid for a new one! This deception on Cary's part was verified by an independent mechanic, as the transmission continued to give us trouble.

I sent the coach back to Cary and demanded that he fix it. Weeks went by and the bus seemed to be missing. Cary's Mobile informed me that they'd had to take it to the following places: Carmenita Ford in La Mirada and Fox Service Center in Fullerton. Because Cary had the bus for so long, we became suspicious about the story and dispatched my manager, Jesse, to verify that the bus was at one of the locations. To our surprise, the bus had never been to either location!

I spoke to the service department at Carmenita Ford because Cary had told me they'd supplied the new transmission. The man at the service department told me they'd never seen or worked on the bus!

I then contacted Cary, who finally told us where the bus was. It was at his storage yard off Imperial Highway and the 91 Freeway. We went over to rescue the bus and found that the transmission was still leaking fluid. We also noticed the following broken items on the bus: train horn, parking brake, navigation, intercom phone, speedometer, and driving lights. Cary claimed no responsibility for the above items and said he'd had nothing to do with them.

Cary sent out his inept mechanic, who took issue with me when we complained about his behavior. He appeared to be on drugs. We notified Cary about his mechanic's poor behavior while at our bus terminal. He then radioed his mechanic to leave.

The enraged mechanic pulled a knife out of his pocket and waved it around, shouting, "You just got me fired!"

I had three employees there at the time. We finally got him to leave.

Jesse went to pick up parts at Cary's shop but he wouldn't give them to us, claiming they were locked up. Cary then radioed his mechanic and told him to pull the parts off a used Detroit truck and pass them off as new.

Cary charged my card for unauthorized amounts. This guy was a complete crook! I did a chargeback on my credit card. That's when his wife called and berated me. She was furious and threatened to sue me. I told her off and called my lawyer. He sent them a certified letter with pictures of the bogus parts. We never heard from them again.

I was wondering, while I wrote this chapter, whether he was still in business. Shockingly, he is! So, if you need a fleet mechanic in Riverside, California, don't call this guy! His real name rhymes with Cary.

PARTY TRAIN PROM COUGAR

Students from a local high school rented the Party Train for their prom night. I was the driver and went to pick them up at their beautiful home in the Harbor. I was early and parked the Train out front.

The mom greeted me and seemed surprised that I was the driver. I had my hair down and looked like Van Halen from the "Hot for Teacher" video. I was even wearing the hat! The teens thought I was cool and the flirty cougar invited me in to eat.

However, food wasn't the only thing on her mind as she started giving me a tour of her home. Thinking about my tip, I was polite and went along with it. When we arrived at the master bedroom, she told me she was divorced and that she liked guys with long hair. Taken aback by how aggressive she was, I started back downstairs. As we descended the stairs together, her daughter caught us and smirked.

I headed back to the bus to load the teens. During the ride, I got a call from the mom, asking how the night was going, creating another opportunity for her to flirt with me. I played it cool but started to worry about the drop-off portion of the night. I just knew this lady would be up waiting.

Sure enough, as I pulled up to the house, the primary was out front greeting the kids. She came over to the bus and wanted to do a walkthrough. Ensuring that nothing was left on board, I walked through the interior with her. It appeared that she had changed her clothes for me and was wearing a sexier outfit.

I admit it was flattering, but I'm married and wasn't about to drive any more passengers that night! LOL. As she approached one of the stripper poles, she showed me her dance moves. As I stood there for her performance, I made a polite gesture and told her I needed to leave. She walked over and gave me a big, long hug and a kiss on the cheek. I was able to fight off her advances and I received my tip in paper money that night!

***NOTE:** A company in Las Vegas bought The Party Train. They drove down, picked her up, and drove her back. I found out that they'd taken down the bulkhead divider. I'm not sure why they did this but now the passengers can walk into the cockpit. This is a bad situation for any driver. It's simply too much of a distraction while one is trying to operate a 60-foot bus! Nevertheless, the Party Train is now servicing the Vegas area.*

The Land Yacht 2.0

The Land Yacht 2.0 is a 1999 Neoplan AN460-articulation bus, the sister bus to the Party Train, and purchased at the same time from the Houston Metro Transit Authority. Mechanically, the only difference between the two buses is the engine. The Land Yacht 2.0 has a Detroit V8-92 engine while the Party Train has a Cummins M11 engine.

I wanted to make the Land Yacht roomier, so I built a smaller bathroom and bar area. My interior had to hold as many people as possible. At one point, we had 115 passengers on the Land Yacht 2.0.

The interior consisted of two dance poles, one in each car. It had speakers throughout the bus and parameter limo-style seating with benches in the center joint, the portion of the bus that bends. I'd often tell clients that this was the best place to sit on the bus. There's a secret optical illusion when you sit there. If the bus is in a turn, you will completely lose sight of the other passengers. It's really two buses in one, and you're seated between them. It was truly a unique experience!

DEATH OF A DRIVER

Finding drivers for the three giant bend buses in our lineup was no easy task. The Land Yacht, Party Train, and Land Yacht 2.0 were very intimidating buses to operate. I wasn't always available to drive and my wife didn't really want me to. She'd miss me on those nights. I'd most definitely rather be out on the town with her than babysitting drunks. My absence would be forgiven in the morning as I plunked $12,000 in cash on the kitchen table. Not a bad take for the weekend!

This money was well-earned, as I had to orchestrate many miraculous tasks to bring the PartyLounge to full power, giving 100 percent of my efforts all week long.

Caring for eight buses while managing drivers, bartenders, and clients was a full-time job. After building the buses and the business from the ground up, I had such duties as marketing, web design, secretarial work, accounting, training, human resources, cleaning the buses, repairing the interiors, maintenance, and doing exterior washes. I even had to evacuate the bathrooms at dump stations.

I managed to snag my newest driver, "Cal," from the local municipal bus company. I needed him to work for me on the weekends when the fleet was booked. Cal drove bend buses for the city during the week. I took him on a test drive and he seemed to know what he was doing. His licensing checked out, he passed a physical, and my insurance cleared him. I was in a real jam to hire this guy fast. Two drivers had just quit on me and one had died. I was blindsided by all of this and in a panic. I had only a week to get PartyLounge back up to full strength.

My driver, Tony, passed away unexpectedly. He was the first person of color to work for me and the first person on my staff to pass away. I was shocked and saddened by the loss but had no time to grieve, as my week was quickly turning into a disaster.

Tony was a very nice guy and a great driver. He was the only person to drive the original Land Yacht besides me. You needed testicular fortitude to get behind the wheel of that behemoth!

He and I worked together on occasion. He'd be the driver and I'd be in the back as the bartender. No other drivers in my staff wanted anything to do with the Land Yacht. The loss of Tony meant I'd be the driver for the rest of her bookings going forward.

"Dimm" and "Witt" quit on me at the end of their Saturday shift. I had no idea until the following Monday. They left signed resignation letters on the driver's seats in their buses. They didn't even have the decency to call me!

They'd been tainted by another driver who turned out to be cancerous to my staff. He was jealous and wanted to be me. I'll call him Bobert. Instead of getting paid an hourly wage, he felt he should be getting a percentage of what I made. Hmm, I never saw his check for the buy-in! He also wanted to be paid from pier to pier. However, I couldn't charge my clients for that. No limo company does this.

He was paid $25 per hour cash with a guaranteed $100 bonus from me. If the client happened to tip him, he got to keep that as well. Sadly, this wasn't good enough for Bobert, Dimm, or Witt. Sounds like the name of a Groupon law firm! LOL.

Bobert refused to take orders, clean his bus, call his clients, or take any responsibility for all his screw-ups. He had an excuse for everything. I gave him many chances. Bobert eventually convinced Dimm and Witt to screw me by quitting a week before a fully booked weekend, causing me to cancel reservations, as well as lose money and reputation.

I couldn't understand how they could quit on me after I'd treated and paid them extremely well. They'd gotten some bad information that they could make more money elsewhere. So, they went to work for another party bus company named P.O.S., aka, "Piece of Shit."

Not wanting to strand hundreds of passengers, I quickly hired two drivers. Cal took the Land Yacht 2.0. I hired his friend for Party Train and I took the Original Land Yacht. It was a super-busy weekend, but I'd made it through!

A month later, Dimm and Witt called me up looking for their old jobs back. I was in disbelief at their hubris.

I said, "You guys quit and you want your job back?"

They explained that P.O.S. Party buses didn't pay them more and that they'd been lied to. It turned out their buses weren't maintained or cleaned. They had to deal with breakdowns and interior equipment failures. P.O.S. would also lock their guests out of the bus bathrooms and then have the drivers charge to open the door. They weren't paid in cash, or even paid that night, as they were accustomed to. They were also expected to clean and fuel their own coaches.

I was laughing on the other end of the phone when I heard all of this. Dimm and Witt claimed that they hadn't quit!

I said, "Hmm, well now. I've got a signed letter from the two of you. I accepted your resignations and have already rehired people to take your place! Not sure how you two fell out of the stupid tree and managed to hit every branch on the way down!" Then I hung up on them. I don't have time for such foolishness!

I never saw them again but heard through other drivers that they continued to bad mouth me. What a shame to have put so much time, effort, and money into staffers who have zero loyalty or appreciation.

I recently checked on P.O.S. Party Buses and am happy to report they're out of business!

THE WONG WAY DRIVER

The Land Yacht 2.0 was booked for a prom in Dana Point Harbor, a difficult place to get in and out of. We'd been there many times before. However, this was my driver Wong Ping's first visit.

The pickup was at the Strand, which was appropriately named. I got a frantic call from Wong.

"I'm stranded at the Strand!" he said.

This was bad timing as I, too, was on the road. It was hard to quarterback my business from the driver's seat! Always multitasking, I wore a headset. It allowed me to answer calls and keep two hands on the wheel. Wong explained that he had gone into the Strand and that it was in a cul-de-sac. Had he followed my instructions and looked up the address on Google Earth, he wouldn't be stuck.

I routinely instructed all of my drivers to pre-select their routes. This way, they wouldn't get the bus stuck. Following the GPS should be the driver's last resort. It has been my experience that GPS systems can get you lost, take you in circles, and put the bus into cul-de-sacs. For that reason, I always instructed my drivers to look up their destinations on a computer prior to driving. However, many of my drivers failed to take direction—pun intended—and then called me to bail them out.

Wong explained that he had taken the Land Yacht 2.0 into a gated community to turn around the bus. The farther he went in, the worse he made the situation. Bend buses like the Land Yacht don't belong in condominium complexes. The Land Yacht is 60 feet long. Wong had managed to jackknife the bus and it was stuck. At the time, I was driving my bus through L.A.—too far away for me to rescue him in Orange County.

I called the driver of Future Lounge, who was servicing the same prom as the Land Yacht. He'd just dropped off his group at the dance and was only a mile from the Land Yacht. I told him to pick up the Land Yacht's passengers and get them to

Party Lounge - The Ride is Over!

their dance. He'd have to make two trips, as his bus held only 40 passengers, and there were 80 teens on the Land Yacht.

As I was trying to organize the rescue, I was flooded with frantic calls from the passengers and parents. They were threatening me with lawsuits, bad Yelp reviews, etc. I tried to tell them that the more they kept me on the phone, the less I could do to remedy the situation. I was still driving my own bus at the time. The music was so loud, it was hard to hear on the phone, even with my headset on. I eventually found a place to pull over.

The rescue bus arrived at the scene and all the kids emptied out of the Land Yacht. Nobody wanted to be left behind, nor did they want the bus to make two trips. So, they managed to pack all 80 teens into the Future Lounge. I still have no idea how they all fit! My driver described it as a clown bus. The doors could barely close, and every inch of room was taken. There were even kids packed into the bathroom and cockpit. Luckily, they had only a mile to go.

The teens were off to their dance but driver Wong Ping was now facing another problem—his bus was blocking the entrance. Seeing the number on the side of the bus, the residents started calling me. They couldn't get in or out of the neighborhood. This was one time when my marketing backfired on me! How I wished they'd stop calling!

I sent Hoss to rescue the Land Yacht. He was a senior supervisor and trainer for the OC Transit Authority. He knew bend buses well. They had only a few hours before the dance was over and the clock was ticking!

Hoss boarded the Land Yacht 2.0 and quickly realized that the bus was in lockout mode. He called me and I directed him to a hidden button above the driver's seat. I knew every bus layout and could visualize the dashboard, stereo, or anything else on board if need be. He found the override button and flipped it. The bus began to maneuver again. Hoss was very good at backing and managed to get the bus straightened out. He got the bus turned around just in time to pick up the teens. The next Monday, I'd received no calls from parents, kids, or neighbors! Another tough weekend on the books!

THE SUSHI BAR PARTY BUS

I love sushi and had a great idea to make a Sushi Party Bus. This idea would save people time and add convenience to their evening. I knew a talented sushi chef. He was starting a side business doing private parties, so I asked him to come out to my bus terminal to discuss my idea. He liked the idea and loved the thought of having his own sushi bar on my bus. He told me exactly what was needed. I built the sushi bar in the back of the Land Yacht.

I bought fast food trays from a restaurant wholesaler and stocked the bus with them. This way, I could sell a package deal, which would include dinner and the ride, effectively turning the bus into the destination. I used this in my marketing. It was printed on my cards, which read, "PartyLounge: Now Going to the Party is the Party!"

The chef would show up at my bus terminal an hour before departure to prep for the meal service. Passengers would board the bus and I'd hand them a tray as they formed a line to the sushi bar.

My first gig came. The waitress, Kristine, and I were servers. Another staffer drove the bus. Kristine, the chef, and I worked as a team throughout the food service. It was amazing to see everyone so excited to be on board. There was no other experience like it! Kristine was the perfect stereotype for all the blonde jokes. She looked like an adult film star and the male customers were very happy to see her on board. Sometimes she'd even get on the stripper pole, causing many fights between couples. Kristine really liked to interact with the customers. She'd even drink with them, which was a problem because she couldn't hold her liquor and the male customers were constantly trying to take her home. There were a few instances when Kristine accidentally dropped trays of food on the customers and even fell into the birthday cake. The female who rented the coach wasn't amused with Kristine when she stood up and had cake stuck to her butt. I quickly defused the situation by letting the primary know that Kristine generally jumped out of cakes, not into them! The guys had a good laugh but the client wasn't having it, and I'd hear from her the very next day. She never rented the bus again! For future serving gigs onboard the sushi bus, I had to defer to another waitress who was far less attractive but who never spilled food or drinks on the customers!

The competition caught wind of my endeavor and started calling state agencies on me. They wanted the Sushi Bus shut down! However, there was no licensing for what I was doing. It was a combination of a catering truck and party bus. I often found myself coming up with ideas for businesses that nobody had ever thought of. So, of course, there would be no licensing or regulations. I figured, nothing ventured, nothing gained. So, I just rolled with it, pun intended!

The Sushi Party Bus was quickly becoming a big earner, so my competition turned me into A.B.C. (Alcohol Beverage Control). They told me that I could no longer serve food and that I needed a license for liquor. I asked them to show me the law for what they were telling me. Of course, they couldn't. I was stuck arguing with them for weeks. They threatened me with jail, impounding, and fines.

I explained to them that I didn't need a liquor license because clients supplied their own liquor! As you'd expect, this concept took days to absorb. A.B.C. was now focused on the food. They told me we couldn't be a mobile restaurant, only a party bus.

Discouraged by the news but not one to quit, I tried to hold onto the concept. However, they were keeping tabs on me and threatened to impound the coach. I was forced to stop advertising the service. The Sushi Party Bus would serve its last meal but the memory would last forever.

Throughout the years, clients would call asking for the service. It was very sad that I couldn't give them what they wanted. Had the government found a way to monetize it, you know there would have been a license or permit to hold.

However, my ideas were so far into the future that the government had no way of keeping up with people like me. Not being one to wait around, I just acted on it until they said "no." Cheers to the Sushi Party Bus. There was no other before or after you!

NOTE: *The Land Yacht 2.0 was bought by the same company that purchased the Party Train. They lost the titles to both buses and reached out to me to fix their problem. I eventually helped them even though they didn't want to pay me.*

I found out that they parked the Land Yacht 2.0 and never used her. They eventually put the bus up for sale on eBay. I had a buyer for them and put the two parties together. The buyer went to pick up the bus but the current owner in Vegas had screwed up the bus's computer and it wouldn't run. The new buyer called me and I told him to leave that bus right where he found it! Once they left my care, all bets were off!

The Perfect Storm

The night started out with our best friends, whom we call "The Bigs." We've known them since I started PartyLounge. Mr. Big was my neighbor and is six-foot-five. Mrs. Big is six-foot-three, while my wife and I are in the five-foot range. Any time we'd enter an establishment, we attracted all the attention. Hanging out with them was always a blast! We were all seated at the bar and drinks were flowing.

Friday night was the kickoff to a very busy weekend. My driver called from the Dream-Lounge and reported that the bus wouldn't air up. I was hoping he'd just made a mistake, as Dream-Lounge was my most reliable bus. I walked out of the bar and continued the call. As I walked him through the startup procedure, I heard an alarm coming from the cockpit. I recognized that sound as the low-air-pressure warning.

Dream's air dryer was making a hissing sound and I knew that wasn't good. I asked the driver to read the air pressure gauge. The bus had only 60 PSI when it should have been at around 125 PSI. That's why the dashboard alarm was on. He didn't have enough air in the suspension to get off the curb. I knew he was truly in trouble.

Things got worse from there. Dream was parked curbside at a prom in Yorba Linda, California when all the teens walked up, wanting to board.

I went from having a good time and buzzed to dead sober in seconds. The first thing I had to do was find a rescue bus. I had to leave the party and get a ride to my home office. Once there, I located one of my coaches. It had cleared for the night and was available to assist. I immediately dispatched the Future Lounge.

I thought I was in the clear but a call came in 20 minutes later. The Future Lounge had broken down halfway en route to rescue the Dream Bus. I just couldn't believe this night!

Then I contacted the driver of the Mega-Lounge, which was still on location at the same dance as Dream Bus. The Mega-Lounge double-decker was picking up her passengers and the driver said there was room for the Dream's passengers.

Knowing the kids didn't want to share the coach, I had to order the driver to divide the two parties. One group would go upstairs and the other downstairs. I figured that because they all attended the same school, they'd be willing to tolerate each other. However, that wouldn't be the case. I had parents calling me, stating that this was unacceptable.

I responded by saying, "Would you rather they be stranded at the event? Why wouldn't you want your kids to help their fellow classmates?"

Well, this client turned out to be a five-star tool bag. She ended up complaining all night long about how we'd handled the situation and she wrote me a bad Yelp review. I guess she'd rather I stranded the kids. I did everything in my power to bring everybody home. Clients like this are truly classless!

"The Mighty Mega-Lounge" is what I called her after that night. She went from a 60-passenger coach to a 90-

passenger coach. She was so grossly overweight but I sent the coach out into the night to avoid leaving kids stranded on prom night ... and it, too, broke down!

Mega's driver called me and stated that the bus was losing air and was leaning to the starboard side. I told him to pull over to examine the rear tag axle. From what the driver was indicating, I determined that the weight of all the kids had blown a hole in the passenger-side airbag, causing the air to leak and causing her to lean to the right.

I told the driver to put the coach in high idle mode while parked. This maneuver was out of sheer desperation and was the bus equivalent of a Hail Mary! High idle mode should build up enough air pressure to release the brakes and get the coach moving again. The gamble worked and Mega was able to continue on her way.

The driver would need to repeat the process of parking and high idling to keep the bus aired up and running. It also kept her on surface streets, as the coach could be operated no faster than 25 miles per hour. It was a long night for Mega but she managed to get everyone home!

Stuck at my office, I got yet another call. This time, it was the Party Train. Her driver reported he had suddenly lost power. Train was loaded with 100 teens and was coming home from another prom. With the Mega-Lounge down, the Dream Bus out of commission, and the Future Lounge stranded in some parking lot, no rescue would be coming. The mobile mechanic was en route to Future Lounge.

I called the driver to the Land Yacht but he was still in San Diego, way out of range for a rescue. Knowing that no other company could possibly accommodate 100 passengers, my only option was to try to fix the bus myself. I loaded up with water and coffee, hopped in my Battle Van, and drove off to the Party Train.

When I arrived on the scene, the driver and passengers were all panicked. I was getting calls from the parents, wanting to know what I was going to do about the situation.

Meanwhile, my mobile mechanic was just arriving at the location where the Future Lounge had broken down. At that point, I literally had to be in three places at the same time. My only stroke of luck was that the Mega-Lounge had managed to make it back to my bus terminal. That left me with just three coaches to retrieve, fix, and get road-worthy by the next evening! If not, I'd be stranding hundreds of passengers and losing thousands of dollars! The pressure was on!

The Party Train's interior limo lights were off and the engine had stopped. Trying not to panic, I checked the most obvious things first. With a quick prayer and the sign of the cross, I went into the engine bay. I spotted two tripped breakers coming from the auxiliary battery. I reset them and the main chassis breakers. Once in the cockpit, I noticed that the bus starter was in the wrong position. This was an easy problem for a driver to cause. He could click the knob one notch over and the bus engine would shut off. With the engine off, the batteries wouldn't have enough power, causing the breakers to pop. With everything in reset, I attempted to restart the bus. It roared back to life and all the lights came on! The passengers were cheering and my driver gave me a high-five! Train was fixed and on her way again.

I then sped down the highway en route to Future Lounge. I arrived at an undisclosed commercial parking lot just off the

55 Freeway in Santa Ana. I found Future Lounge parked in a pool of her own oil. A security guard approached me, very upset about the mess. He expected me to clean it all up and get the bus out of there. However, I wasn't equipped to clean such a large mess. The oil slick went all the way through the parking lot and led out to the street.

I told him the bus had broken down and couldn't be moved. He continued to threaten me and called the police. I just drove off in search of cleaning supplies. The last thing this night needed was a security guard with an attitude!

I found a nearby Home Depot and put together a makeshift hazmat spill kit. When I arrived back on the scene, my mechanic told me the bad news. The bus would have to be towed. The problem with that was, not many companies had the equipment to do the job. I needed a tow yard with a Landoll truck. That would be the only way to flatbed a 40-foot bus.

I started calling companies and finally found one that agreed to take on the job at the cost of $1,000. They wouldn't be on the scene for several hours. I decided to use that time to clean the parking lot. The mechanic stayed behind and gave me a hand. The oil spill was substantial and took a total of three hours to clean up. The security guard mad-dogged us the entire time. I feverishly worked until the tow truck driver finally arrived a full three-and-a-half hours after I'd called them. I was exhausted when he pulled up.

Assessing the situation, the tow driver informed me that he wouldn't be willing to steer the bus as it was pulled onto the flatbed. The only way he'd agreed to do the tow was if I'd steer the bus as he pulled it in. I had no choice and quickly hopped into the cab. The bed of the truck rose into the air at a steep angle. It began pulling the bus onto the flatbed. There was only one inch on either side of the truck bed. Future Lounge took up the entire width. One false move and she'd fall off the truck. It was precision steering at its finest! The Future Lounge was lifted in the air in a vertical position that made the bus look like it was about to take flight! The bed of the truck dropped to the horizontal position and my job was done. It was a terrifying maneuver!

After the Future Lounge was towed back to our bus terminal, it was on to the Dream Bus. We arrived at the bus on Saturday morning. I'd been working through the night and was running out of time and energy. The mobile mechanic looked at the coach. He found that the air regulator valve had been stuck in the "open" position, forcing the air out of the tanks. He was able to fix it on location and I drove her back to my yard.

After that, I went home for a few hours of sleep. That morning, I returned to my bus terminal with the mobile mechanic. We worked on repairs to the Mega-Lounge and Future Lounge all day. We managed to get them fixed in time for their Saturday night gigs. I was still at my bus yard cleaning up the interiors when my drivers started arriving at night.

My clients had no idea how close they'd been to having no transportation. I've never worked harder and longer to take care of my business.

My Lost TV Show

PIMP MY RV WITH CAPTAIN MARKY MARK

In 2012, I received a call from Nancy Glass Productions. They wanted to know if I was the guy who built RV limousines.

I said, "Yes, I'm the Captain!"

The lady started laughing. She told me they were developing a show about RV conversions and were interested in casting me. They set up a Skype meeting with me the next day.

Skyping from my home office was perfect. It looks like a pirate bar and gift shop! The producers were very amused. I was in full character, wearing my PartyLounge shirt and hat.

The interview went very well. I told them that if they signed me, I'd open my files and help them with character development, dialog, storyboarding, and casting. They loved my enthusiasm and willingness to help. I also mentioned that I'd archived files from my business and that I was willing to sell my stories and write shows.

A week went by. I was on pins and needles waiting for them to call with a decision. I received an email with the contract. They'd officially signed me to the show. I received a congratulatory call and was so excited, I could barely contain myself.

The producers requested that I put together a cast and then set up another Skype meeting. I immediately called a few people I already had in mind. The Skype meeting with my hand-picked cast and I went very well. I thought for sure they'd be signed, too. Things seemed to be moving along, as the producers and I were in contact daily.

The show was to be named, "Pimp My RV with Captain Marky Mark." Because I was signed to the show, I gave them my full commitment. I opened my files and shared my intellectual rights. I wanted the show to be a complete success!

A few weeks went by and I hadn't heard from the producers. I reached out to them and they said everything was fine. A month went by and still nothing. I contacted them again. They said they were just shopping the show around.

Six weeks later, one of my castmates contacted me. He'd seen an article online advertising our show. However, the name had been changed to "Rock My RV with Bret Michaels." My show had been picked up by the Travel Channel.

I called up Nancy Glass Productions and they confirmed that the show had moved on without me. They explained that the Travel Channel wanted talent with a big name as the lead. I told them they were making a huge mistake. Viewers weren't going to believe a singer was now a bus designer. This gave the show no merit or longevity!

I had an IMDB (Internet Movie Database) profile at the time and a good reputation. I had appeared in the 1993-1994 episodes of Saban's "Mighty Morphin Power Rangers." The show originated in Japan. I was signed with Charles Mathews Talent agency to be the Red Ranger stunt man. Being the tough guy in the red suit was fun! I got to fight all the silly monsters and was fed well, too. The filming days were long, some lasting up to 18 hours. We had to show up at different locations throughout Southern California. One famous filming location was the Bronson Cave in Los Feliz, located below the Griffith Observatory in Los Angeles. It was difficult finding all those filming locations, as there was no GPS and no cell phones back then!

I also appeared on these shows: MTV's "Next," "Sunset Tan," "Elimidate," "Famously Single," and "The Tonight Show." I had my own website media and marketing campaign. I advertised on the sides of all my buses. I designed custom shirts as well as business cards that clipped to the rim of one's drink. I created marketing videos for the PartyLounge YouTube Channel. I sold merchandise on my website. I even had my own TV commercial on Time Warner Cable. Apparently, that wasn't good enough for them. They couldn't care less and offered me no apologies!

I couldn't believe they'd break their own contract and I investigated the idea of suing them. My childhood friend, who is an entertainment lawyer, told me it would cost hundreds of thousands to litigate. That's how studios get away with stealing your ideas!

I was super disappointed and felt completely violated! After a few episodes, just as I predicted, the show tanked! It just goes to show how frail and narrow-minded Hollywood can be. I fully expect to have my own show after this book blows up. That's when the Travel Channel and Nancy Glass Productions will be kicking themselves!

The TV Shows

My marketing was in full swing. PartyLounge was getting the notoriety that I'd worked so hard to achieve. I'd received a phone call from a network out of Warner Brothers studios. They were interested in seeing the Pirate Hopper. They'd offered to give me and the bus a spot in a new reality TV show called "Elimidate." So, I went to Hollywood to meet with the producers. They explained that I'd be filming the pilot episode and would be using the Pirate Hopper as the platform on which the TV show would be filmed. "Elimidate" was a TV show about singles who would meet for the first time. One contestant would decide whether to eliminate one of the singles as the date progressed. The premise was that, as the singles were eliminated, one person would be left for the main contestant to be with. These dates would take the coach to different locations throughout Hollywood. As the driver, I'd have to interact with the contestants only when they were on the bus. If they'd been eliminated, they'd remain on the bus with me but would no longer be on camera.

These TV shows took a long time to film. Seeing that I was the driver and the owner of the coach, the network had promised me money, fame, and future business. I'd find out that none of it was true. I was told that my name, the company name, our phone number, and our website address would all be used in the credits. This was to be a form of payment. The producers felt that I'd be getting so much business for PartyLounge, they didn't need to pay me anything out of pocket.

It took weeks of my time to get the coach ready for filming. I had to bring the coach up to Hollywood from Huntington Beach and stay with it while they rigged the bus with cameras and lighting. They also had to rig it for sound. They even had a special sound guy with a mixing board set up in front of the coach next to the driver's seat. This made it extremely hard to drive the vehicle. With the filming going on, it became very difficult and distracting to get the coach through the busy streets of Hollywood.

One day, during filming, a car pulled out in front of the bus, causing me to jam on the brakes. We narrowly avoided an accident. The driver of the pickup truck flipped us off and stayed in the middle of Sunset Boulevard. We came to such an abrupt stop that the contestants, the camera guy, and the soundboard had all hit the ground, as they weren't seat-belted in. I was so mad that I flew out of the coach to confront this redneck and his reckless driving. We started to wrestle, and the producers, the contestants, the camera guys, and the sound guy all came out to pull me from him. After the melee was over, Redneck abruptly got in his pickup truck and sped off. I was still heated and asked them if they'd gotten it on tape. They said they had but wouldn't be using it in the TV show. I told them that it was a huge mistake; this was the kind of thing people tuned in for. I thought to myself, *What a missed opportunity for these producers.* Nowadays, you can go to YouTube and see this type of road rage all the time, most of which is staged.

In the coming days, the contestants began to really bond with me. However, every episode had new contestants. I found myself liking some more than others. I even stay in contact with one of them today. She's a very nice girl and I gave her a spot on my party bus, as cocktail waitresses—specifically, good-looking girls with good work ethics who possessed a fun, friendly attitude—were hard to come by. During this filming, my regular cocktail waitresses had asked to be on the show with me.

NEXT

Another TV show I did was MTV's "Next," which was a lot like "Elimidate." It seemed to me that these producers were running out of ideas and were ripping each other off by renaming the same show. I told them I had plenty of great ideas; however, they wouldn't listen to me. The result was that these TV shows had no longevity. The producers' shortsightedness, combined with the studio's thriftiness, made for a one-and-done season.

In MTV's "Next," I spent more time on the bus. It eventually spun off to a different show, "The 5th Wheel." This was also a dating show, and this time the party bus was used 100 percent of the time rather than as only part of the date. As usual, I was promised that, if the show got picked up by a network, my bus would be used. This, too, was a lie. The network picked up the show and used a totally different bus and company.

Working with Hollywood producers was starting to weigh on me. I'd get calls from network producers and wouldn't even bother returning them. They always wanted me to do something for nothing and their shows required 18-hour workdays. Sometimes they'd take weeks to complete. For example, MTV wanted me to stay on location for a couple of weeks straight. They put me in a hotel in Santa Monica, gave me a personal assistant, and had another driver take my coach to their lot, where it was locked down for the night. MTV had given me a small allowance from which I was able to eat and charge to the show. However, at the end of filming, they refused to pay for the hotel food that I'd ordered for the two-week stay. I'd constantly have to haggle with them over the expenses or threaten to take the coach and go home, which would have stopped filming for the day.

They'd rigged the coach so haphazardly that one morning, when I got in it, the wires had caught on fire and the cabin was filled with smoke while parked in the MTV lot. I had only one fire extinguisher with which to douse all the glowing, red-hot wires underneath the dashboard. I was coughing and choking as I made my way out of the coach but I could still see that the wires were about ready to ignite again. This time, I had no fire extinguisher left to battle any additional flames. So, I ran back in there, prayed to God to save the coach, stuck my hand into the hot wire harness, and ripped it out, giving myself second-degree burns in the process.

After the ordeal, the producer called, demanding that I bring the coach to the film location. I tried to explain to him that the coach had just been on fire as a direct result of all the freaking rigging they'd done to it the night before. Most of the systems onboard were destroyed, yet somehow the Pirate Hopper was able to be started. So, I drove the coach to the film location minus the headlights, turn signals, running lights, brake lights, and taillights. Apparently, all those wire leads had burned up in the fire.

At the film location, the producers boarded the Pirate Hopper and started complaining about the smoke. I told them there was nothing I could do about it and that the coach was lucky to be there, as it had almost just burned down. I showed them my hand, which was burned from the wires, and they had a medic bandage me up. Then they had their PA send me to an automotive store, where we bought tools, wiring, and other accessories necessary for me to make the repairs. As the producers were setting up the next scene for the show, I was busy repairing the Pirate Hopper. I managed to get the headlights back online.

I had to walk away from the coach for a few minutes to catch my breath because it still smelled like smoke. That's when a street sweeper came down the cul-de-sac with the ticketing truck. I ran back to the Hopper and tried to start it but it was flooded and wouldn't turn over. The street sweeper went around us, while the ticketing truck stopped and began writing me a ticket. I tried to explain to him that I was part of the TV show filming across the street and that I'd parked the coach over here to work on it and get it out of the scene. The officer wasn't buying my story, as he didn't believe the Pirate Hopper was part of any TV show. We started arguing and got loud. This got the attention of the producers, who ran over to my defense. They finally convinced the officer that I was part of the production.

I got the Pirate Hopper started and was able to drive it back onto the location site. The contestants boarded and we drove the coach over to West Hollywood. When we got to West Hollywood, there was no catered location, nor was there craft service. The producers decided to take the crew and the talent out to lunch. The crew was to eat first, so I, being the driver and the talent, stayed on board the Pirate Hopper. The talent was getting restless and bored, as the day was taking forever and they weren't getting paid. I told them that I had liquor on board because this was, in fact, a working party bus. Everybody wanted to have a drink to lower their inhibitions. I thought it was a great idea, as the show was moving very slowly and getting the talent buzzed would make for better programming. What I didn't know was that some of the talent had live microphones and the executive producer was listening. She ran over to the Pirate Hopper, opened the door, and started screaming at me in front of the talent. She ordered me off the bus.

She was a big woman and very intimidating. She screamed, "How can you let these people drink on the TV show? You know they're not supposed to be doing that!" I told her I'd forgotten MTV's rules and that everyone had only one drink. She was still yelling at me and was threatening to have me thrown off the TV show. I told her, "Fine, I'll go and I'll take my bus with me."

Now it seemed the shoe was on the other foot. She started backing down as she realized that if I left, they were going to be shut down for the day. For the remainder of the film shoot, the executive producer and I didn't get along or even talk to each other. Because they were treating me so poorly, I decided to take my wife out to an expensive dinner on them, charging it to my hotel room. When I checked out of the hotel room, my credit card wasn't on file; rather, it was the studio's card. That's what they get for trying to screw with the Captain!

SUNSET TAN

This TV show had it all: a cast of narcissistic, self-indulgent, entitled, up-and-coming wannabe starlets and the guys who wanted to bang them. I remember receiving the call from the producers while walking through a casino in Las Vegas. Hollywood was calling and I should have known better than to answer. When Hollywood called, it was always about what I could do for them. I wanted nothing to do with another dead-end TV show.

The caller's name was Kat, and she started off nice enough. She was able to build a rapport with me to the point that she sparked my interest. Yet, I still had the hesitation of someone who wanted to hang up. She promised all the usual things, such as having my name in the credits and showing my phone and web address. I told her I'd been down this road before and it wouldn't be enough to get me to be a part of any more TV shows. I had to get paid. If they didn't want to do that, they could find another coach. She explained that they didn't want just any coach; they wanted the mighty Mega-Lounge double-decker party bus. Because there were no other double-decker party buses in California, it seemed that I had them over a barrel. We started negotiating a price and they told me what the show's budget was for transportation.

The idea was to have me pick up the talent at some mansion in Beverly Hills. They also wanted me to be the driver, accompanied by two of my cocktail waitresses. After arriving at a monetary crossroads, I decided to do the show. I got the Mega-Lounge ready and planned to be gone from sunup to sundown. I called my waitress, Anna, who agreed to be on the show along with my wife, Mickey. I had both girls wear the traditional PartyLounge tank top. The girls and I drove out to Hollywood and got to the bottom of a big hill called Mount Olympus. I'd explained to the producers that I wasn't certain whether the double-decker would be able to traverse the narrow, steep streets of Beverly Hills. They insisted that the coach would make it, no problem. That's when I knew I was in trouble.

We started up the first big hill and had to dodge many tree branches. The double-decker wasn't made to be on streets like that. To make matters worse, the mansion was in a cul-de-sac. We went around hairpin turns and were able to squeeze by all the parked cars on these extraordinarily narrow streets. As we got to the very last street, I had to get out of the Mega-Lounge and walk to the end of the cul-de-sac to see if there was any way to turn the bus around. There was no visible way to perform a U-turn on that street, so I had to back the coach in. This required backing around tree branches and parked cars, going around corners, and even squeezing between cars to get the double-decker up to the mansion's front door. The crew came out and immediately started working on Mega, wiring it for microphones and cameras, and even setting up a scene. The talent came out to see the bus, took one look at it, turned around, and walked back in, never once acknowledging the waitresses or me.

Just as I was getting ready to take some direction from the producers, a neighbor walked onto the set and started yelling at me for leaving a fuel trail from the bottom of the hill, past his house, through two streets, and over into the cul-de-sac. Apparently, the steep hill had caused the diesel tanks of the double-decker to overflow from a tube in the back of the engine. I didn't know they were there. Their specific purpose was in case the fuel tanks had been overfilled. It seemed that we were in big trouble before the film day even started. The producers managed to get some people to clean up the mess and calm down the homeowner. All I wanted to do was get the hell out of there, realizing that I'd have to bring them back and do it all over again in the dark.

The producers brought the talent out of the mansion while being filmed. They showed me helping them aboard the coach as I introduced myself and the staff. The women of the show walked by and snubbed every one of us as they headed upstairs. When the cameras weren't rolling, I brought my wife and cocktail waitress, Anna, up there and we all introduced ourselves, trying to establish a rapport with them. However, the girls seemed uninterested in meeting us. I guess a few them had been on some short walk-on parts and thought that they were already big starlets. Their attitudes were so ridiculous, I couldn't imagine working with them for the rest of the day. I dropped off the talent at Dave & Buster's in the Valley. Then I went to fuel the coach. The producers refused to pay for the fuel and I thought, *Here we go again*. This was going to be a long day, as both the talent and the producers were problematic. I went back to Dave & Buster's, where I'd left Mickey and Anna. I ran into some of the talent and attempted to talk to them one more time but they walked right past me. I couldn't get over how rude those bitches were!

The guys from the show were congenial. Later in the evening, the producers called it a wrap, then proceeded to tell me that I was driving them all to dinner in West Hollywood. I said my contract didn't include me being a taxi for the show. Seeing that they weren't going to be paying me extra, I promptly declined, as I didn't want to spend one more minute than I had to with any of them.

The long drive home was in the dark, and I knew that at the end of it I'd be facing a giant hill laced with trees, cars, and an angry neighbor. I'd have to traverse all of this to get the crew and talent home. Then, it was still a two-hour drive to get the girls and me back in traffic that night. When I finally arrived in Huntington Beach, I was exhausted.

I called the producers to get the air date. The show was to start with me picking up the people. However, most of the scenes I was in had been cut and all the scenes the girls were in had been cut! In fact, you could see only the back of me as I was boarding the talent into the coach, and even that was fleeting! Once again, I'd been screwed over by Hollywood! So, I looked for my company name, phone number, and web address to be in the credits as promised. The credits rolled and only the name PartyLounge was in it. I don't know, for the life of me, why these thieving morons tell you one thing and do another. I did my part and, in the end, all they had to do was theirs.

FAMOUSLY SINGLE

I was sitting in my home office when the producers of "Famously Single" called me. It had been several years since I'd done the other shows but I still had a bad taste in my mouth. I basically had the mindset that I'd never do another party bus TV show again. The producers and I talked for several weeks about using the Party Train. We'd reached an agreement that would yield me thousands of dollars at the end of the filming week. Not only that, I didn't have to drive the bus, which would sit parked most of the time. This studio had a lot of money and was doing it all the right way. They pulled the necessary permits for the coach and it was an official production vehicle. I sent my driver to the film location and they used the coach as it was, just parked there. He only had to drive it to one location and back. At the end of the filming week, I was paid my money and had no problems whatsoever. I never did see the airing of that episode and I'm not sure how quickly the show went off the air. I'm assuming it was another one-season production.

PARTYLOUNGE COMMERCIAL

It had always been my dream to have my own TV commercial. I started looking into it and came across an advertisement for late-night television with Time Warner Cable. I gave them a call and they invited me down to their studios for a meeting. Their sales pitch was a lot like being exposed to a timeshare presentation. There was a lot involved in having a commercial on television. We had to go out and shoot it. It had to be edited and formatted, and somebody had to pick out the talent. Time Warner initially wanted tens of thousands of dollars to do all this. A few weeks went by and their agent called to tell me that they could give me a special price if I'd sign with them. I set up another meeting so we could hammer out the details. With all my money wrapped up in the business, shooting a commercial was very aggressive, as I was bankrolling the entire operation myself. I explained to the Time Warner producers that I'd come up with the talent, the vehicle, the film location, and my own photographer. They responded, saying they'd only use their camera crew and would handle all the editing. We were able to come up with a reasonable price to start the production. I'd also have to pay for all the air dates for the commercial. I had a specific budget in mind and was able to convince Time Warner to lower their price. My goal was to be the very first party bus company to have a commercial on TV.

Currently, we're still the first and only party bus commercial ever to air on television in Southern California. I rounded up the talent, which included me, my wife, and three of our sexy friends. We picked the Hustler casino, which was a perfect backdrop for the commercial. I wrote the commercial and we all acted our parts. The commercial was to last for 30 seconds and had to be formatted. Time Warner's production company edited it down to 21 seconds.

I remember seeing it for the first time on TV. I used to love seeing my commercial play. I was so proud and so amazed at how far I'd come in such a short amount of time. I remember running errands and bumping into people who had seen the commercial and who recognized me. The feedback was very amusing. They all thought the commercial was hilarious and they loved all the hot chicks! Overnight, I became a celebrity in my own town! I'd even have people wanting to stop and talk to me at the grocery store! Once, when I was pulled over in my Corvette for speeding down Pacific Coast Highway, the cop recognized me from the commercial. I was able to charm my way out of getting a ticket. My wife was in the car and couldn't believe the performance I gave the cop! I believe she was a little envious, as she'd been unable to duplicate the results when she received a ticket a few months earlier.

The calls came in from the commercial. People wanted the coach to show up at their kids' birthday parties so the adults could drink at the curb. The Pirate Hopper was making some easy money off that commercial. I had lots of fun driving it around even if it wasn't rented out. I figured driving it around like an ad truck in combination with the commercial would give me that one-two punch the business needed. People even wanted to check out the coach while at the gas station. I always let them in and had business cards on hand to give to them. The advertising on the side of the coach was doing so well, I decided to put it on every coach. Standard issue on all PartyLounge buses was my photo, my web address, my phone number, the name of the company, and the name of the bus. This super-terrific branding made the vehicles highly recognizable. When you saw a PartyLounge bus, you knew it!

We had a lot of character, unlike other buses that started copying me. Other companies would just have a number for a bus but my buses had names. I knew my marketing was working when people would call up and ask for a specific bus by name. It always simplified things during the phone process. Teens would call in asking for a favorite bus as if it were their friend.

Stupid Phone Calls and Illegal Party Buses

I spent half of my week in my home office and the other half at my bus terminal. I'd be working on all the different files, coordinating buses with drivers, etc. Scheduling always took up lots of my time. I personally contacted staffers for availability and set up the weekend. Pairing drivers with waitresses was tough because some of the girls didn't like the guys. But all the drivers loved the girls!

I would answer calls by saying, "PartyLounge!" The caller would often reply, "Is this PartyLounge?" Sometimes I'd have to repeat it multiple times! This became very annoying to me. Sometimes I'd just repeat "PartyLounge" over and over until they understood. That's when people would ask, "Is this the party bus company?" Holy cow, I wanted to reach through the phone and punch them in the brain! Once we got past the initial greeting, I'd often think to myself, *Oh my goodness, perhaps you're too stupid to rent a bus from me.*

I knew that when calls started off and we couldn't get past the initial greeting, it would be a long conversation. I often thought, *How long have you been using the phone?* Most of the time, people had no idea what they were asking for. It was as if I were a party planner and buses were from outer space. For the most part, I was extremely patient with callers. However, after I'd answered the phone for 20 years, my composure started to change.

All the ridiculous questions from callers would sometimes take me off my sales pitch. Some calls were so ridiculous, I couldn't help but have fun with them. I'd occasionally speak with phony accents and act silly! Did I mention there's a bar in my office? You'd need one too if you had to answer my phone!

Here are some actual transcripts from a few of my most memorable calls:

(Ring, Ring) Captain: "Hello, PartyLounge."

Caller: "Ahh, yes, is this PartyLounge?"

Captain: "No, it's PartyLounge!"

Caller: "Oh, I'm sorry. I'm looking for PartyLounge."

Captain: "Oh, that's great! This is PartyLounge!"

Caller: "Huh? I'm confused. Is this the party bus company?"

Captain: "Yes, it is!"

Caller: "What's the name of your company?"

Captain: "It's PartyLounge!"

Caller: "Oh."

This was when I poured myself a drink to give the person on the other end enough time to formulate his next brilliant question.

Next Call, (Ring Ring) Captain: "Hello, PartyLounge."

Party Lounge - The Ride is over!

Caller: "Hi, is this the party bus company?"

Captain: "Umm, pretty sure!"

Caller: "How many levels is your double-decker party bus?"

Captain: "Seriously? Five, ma'am, LOL."

Caller: "Five?"

Captain: "Okay, there's actually two."

Caller: "Okay, cool. I didn't want the bus to get stuck under a bridge."

Captain: "Seriously?"

Caller: "Are the stairs on the outside of the bus?"

Captain: "So, you think people are going down the highway on a double-decker bus that has stairs on the outside of it?"

Caller: "Umm, no, I guess not. So, does it have an elevator, then?"

Captain: "Bahahaha, NOOOOO! The stairs are on the inside of the bus, ma'am!"

Caller: "Oh."

(Ring, Ring) Captain: "PartyLounge, how may I help you?"

Caller: How many passengers fit on your 30-passenger bus?"

Captain: "All of them!"

Caller: "Umm, I meant what's your maximum capacity?"

Captain: "Thirty, ma'am."

Caller: "I mean, how many more can we fit in it?"

Party Lounge - The Ride is Over!

Captain: "Thirty passengers is the maximum!"

Caller: "Yes, I understand that, but can we fit an extra five more?"

Captain: "Oh, I get it. You were taught Common Core in high school, weren't you?"

Caller: "Yes, how did you know?"

Captain: "Bahahaha," CLICK!

(Ring, Ring) Captain: "PartyLounge."

Caller: "Ah, yes, how many bathrooms does your bus have?"

Just a side note: When a person calls you and says, "Ah, yes" before they formulate a question, it says volumes about their mental capacity. Is it a nervous tick, like Tourette syndrome? Anyway, back to the call.

Captain: "Just one bathroom, ma'am."

Caller: "Oh, that's a surprise to me."

Captain: "Why is that? Have you been on buses with multiple bathrooms?"

Caller: "Umm, no, but I'm looking for one."

Captain: "Why would you need that?"

The caller hung up at this point. Perhaps she was too embarrassed to continue.

(Ring, Ring) Captain: "PartyLounge."

Caller: "Yo, is this the party bus company?"

Party Lounge - The Ride is Over!

Captain: "Yes, it is. How can I help you?"

Caller: "I'm a club promoter and don't want to be charged by the hour but you'll be making so much money off me because I'm going to rent you every week!"

Captain: "So, how will you be paying?"

Caller: "I'll be paying you a flat rate."

Captain: "What's your budget?"

Caller: "Huh, umm, well, we can get it done for a hundred."

Captain: "No, that's what I charge per hour, not per night."

Caller: "Yeah, but you're going to get so much business from me..."

Captain: "Buddy, what you need is an illegal party bus. I'm definitely not your guy."

Caller: "Oh, but we like your bus."

Captain. "Well, then pay for it. I'm not running a charity here!"

(Ring, Ring) Captain: "PartyLounge."

Caller: "I was on your website and read there's no smoking on your bus. Is that correct?"

Captain: "Yes, no smoking."

Caller: "Why is that? I've smoked on other party buses."

Captain: "My policy is in place for your safety."

Caller: "So, we can't bring in weed?"

Captain: "NO!"

Caller: "Cigars?"

Captain: "NO!"

Caller: "Cigarettes?"

Captain: "What is it you're not getting here?"

Caller: "Well, damn man, I'm going to use another company."

Captain: "Please do, as I don't need my bus to burn down just so your group can hot box in my coach!"

Caller: "Screw you, man!"

Captain: "I don't get down like that." ... Click!

(Ring, Ring) Captain: "PartyLounge."

Caller: "My son and his date were on your bus and they left a few things there."

Captain: "Were they on the high school prom bus or the adult birthday bus?"

Caller: "Well, umm, yes, they were on the prom bus."

Captain: "Oh, wow, so you want to retrieve liquor, panties, and a broken high heel?"

Caller: Click.

(Ring, Ring) Captain: "PartyLounge."

Caller: "Hi, I was on your bus and lost my cutlet. I want to know if you found it?"

Captain: "You mean the cutlet that you stuff your bra with?"

Caller: "Yeah, that's right."

Captain: "Sure, it's here, but you may want to wait a while before coming over."

Caller: "Why is that?"

Captain: "Because I'm still trying to chip it out of our ice bin. It's frozen solid and blocking our drain!"

Caller: Click.

Captain: "Hello? Hello? Ah, she hung up. What a shame! I wanted to see the look on her face when I handed over her chilled silicone boobie!"

(Ring, Ring) Captain: "PartyLounge."

Caller: "My son rented your bus and we want our money back! We're also going to write you a bad review! We're also going to turn you into the state!"

Captain: "Ma'am, your son was caught drinking on my bus and he assaulted my driver!"

Caller: "So? You didn't have to end the ride!"

Captain: "Yes, I did. It was an assault and this is in the contract you signed!"

Caller: "You owe me four thousand dollars!"

Captain: "No, I don't. Your ride was terminated due to your breach of contract."

Caller: I'm going to call the police for grand theft!"

Captain: "Don't bother. I already called them and filed a statement regarding your son. Would you like me to add you to it as well?"

Caller: "I'll get you for this!"

Captain: "F-off, you bitch!"

Caller: "OMG, I can't believe you cursed at me!"

Captain: "Lady, you're the first caller to ever get me to do so!" Click!

After this call, the banter was far from over. This lady had all the kids on the bus write negative reviews about PartyLounge and me. All were lies and had nothing to do with what really happened. The parents of this rental thought it was okay for the kids to drink. However, it's strictly against the law to allow minors to drink.

In fact, four teens had died on the road that night as a result of underage drinking and driving. The kids on my bus had been stopped from drinking. My staff and I had the law on our side. The police had to come out to the bus and separate the angry mob of teenagers from my driver. The police found their liquor and allowed the bus to leave. The parents were mad because they'd had to come pick up the kids. Sad to know that there are so many irresponsible adults like this in the world.

I managed to get five of the eight bad reviews removed from Yelp. I never heard from them again. However, I placed a call to the principal of their high school. He was grateful for my actions and I identified all the students involved, as they'd had to sign into the bus prior to boarding. There was no way for them to deny any of it. I sure hope they got suspended! As for the bad parents, let's hope they don't continue to procreate!

I got calls from people all over the United States.

Apparently, our Orange County service area was confusing them because there are four Orange Counties in the U.S.: California, New York, North Carolina, and Florida. All over my website, just above our phone number, I had indicated that we service Southern California Only! However, that didn't stop all those calls from people who couldn't read!

Out-of-state calls were frequently for Las Vegas. I had to constantly explain to people that we were licensed in California only and couldn't leave the state. For some reason, people think that if you have a bus, you can automatically go anywhere. This isn't the case! To take a passenger to other states, you need to be federally licensed. This is far more complex and expensive than operating in your home state.

I would also receive calls asking me to take the passengers to Mexico or Canada. The most ridiculous out-of-country call came from London, England. A boy wanted my bus for his high school dance. I told him I was in the United States! "How much would I have to charge him for that ride?" he asked. I thought he was joking but, clearly, he wasn't. I was befuddled at the logistics alone!

Another call came from the personal assistant to the owners of the Palace Casinos. They also own the Ultimate Fighting Championship, UFC. They wanted my bus, the Party Train, to do a prom in Las Vegas. I declined, as there would have been too many risks and I would have had to sneak the bus over there. California state licensing was on the side of my bus. Ha! If a Nevada State Trooper caught us transporting passengers who had been picked up from his state, the bus would have been impounded.

I tried to explain this to them, but they wouldn't take no for an answer. They called me for two weeks, begging me to do the job. I told them, "Fine, give me $15,000 and sign a contract stating that you're fully responsible for the bus if it gets fined and/or impounded."

They said no and I was okay with that. Seems to me a billionaire family could have afforded my price!

ILLEGAL PARTY BUSES

Over the years, I encountered many illegal party buses. I called them "pirate buses." When I started this business, there were no such companies. I started noticing them spring up one by one. It was obvious that they were trying to emulate me but they operated with no licensing or insurance. This put the public at risk, as there was no oversight. All their vehicles were in bad mechanical shape. Most of them were made from old, converted airport shuttle vans. They had no restrooms or other amenities that you'd find on the PartyLounge buses.

These companies started interfering with the industry, causing the State of California to pass new regulations, which increased our insurance rates every year. These types of pirate buses were involved in many accidents, thefts, fraud, injuries, and even deaths.

One company I kept my eyes on was exceptionally bad. They called themselves P.E.L. However, they changed their company name multiple times to avoid the law. They were frequently spotted at the same events we serviced. They had no business transporting passengers in those buses! I tried to explain to callers that while this company may have been cheaper than we were, their kids wouldn't be safe. When I couldn't get my point across to clients that you get what you pay for, I had to just let them go in disbelief. It was hard losing business to a one-star company. At the end of the day, it showed me how cheap and irresponsible people would have to be to let their kids take that ride.

I felt bad for the drivers of P.E.L., as they had no idea their boss was a criminal. I tried to explain to them who they worked for, but they'd have to find out for themselves. Several of their employees called me looking for a new job. They remembered me as an owner-operator. I had to rescue them from situations when they got their buses stuck.

I called the State Highway Patrol on them many times, but nothing was ever done to put them out of business. They just kept reappearing as a new company with the same buses. Eventually, they got bad press and made the news. They left 60 adults at a racetrack, stranding them there. That's what happens when a company overbooks and takes your money upfront. Don't expect them to come back for you! This is how P.E.L. operated. They lied to everyone.

Another bad company used to lock their clients out of the bathrooms and then tried to make the passengers pay a fee to unlock the door! My clients told me the horror stories and often thanked me for being so professional. I had many return customers. PartyLounge was a five-star operation.

There's a large bus company on TV that operates out of Hollywood. They took their double-decker charter bus on the freeway for a teen birthday party. Open-top buses aren't allowed on the freeway. However, this company couldn't care less, as it was all about money! One of the teenagers went to the top deck and stood on the seat. He was hit by an overpass sign at 60 miles per hour and was killed instantly. This caused problems for my business, as people were afraid of renting my double-decker bus. I had to explain to potential renters that my second deck is enclosed and can legally be on the freeways. The company that killed the teenager has buses featured on TMZ. I notified the TV show to tell them about what happened and asked why they didn't mention it in any of their episodes. TMZ never got back to me!

Another company, Designer Limousine, which operated a double-decker party bus on the East Coast of the United States, took notice of my bus's name. They started using a similar name, Mega Liner. Unfortunately, because I market the bus with the name Mega-Lounge, people from New Jersey would call asking for the Mega Liner. I told them that my coach was called the Mega-Lounge and that we were located on the West Coast.

Designer Limousine had a teenage party on their bus. A kid went to the top deck, opened the roof hatch, climbed out, and was decapitated by a freeway overpass sign. D.L. took my bus name but not my safety standards. This also made for more confusing calls, as passengers were afraid of my double-decker for no reason! D.L. hadn't replaced the top-deck roof hatch, which passengers constantly tampered with. It's there in case the bus turns over onto its side. It allows people to climb out by just removing a pin.

After losing the entire roof hatch on one of my jobs, I asked the passengers what they'd done. One of them had been trying to smoke and had pulled the pin. To his surprise, the wind had yanked the entire hatch off the roof, leaving a two-by-two-foot hole.

I fixed it the next day by installing a skylight over it. This could easily be kicked out if the bus was turned over but it couldn't be opened when the bus was upright. Had D.L. had this in place, their passenger would still be alive.

The End of an Era

PartyLounge went from fun and lighthearted to extremely difficult to operate. The C.P.U.C., California Public Utilities Commission, was breathing down my neck. Back then, they oversaw licensing for all transportation. They charged a quarterly fee based on our earnings, forcing us to be over-insured while maintaining policies we didn't need.

One such policy was the California State Compensation Insurance Fund. They'd audit us annually, looking for bookkeeping errors and trying to get additional cash from us. I viewed them all as gangsters! It made no sense for

PartyLounge to have a workman's composition policy. All our drivers were independent contractors.

Another annual inspection came from the CHP, California Highway Patrol. Their inspections lasted all day. They'd perform an audit of my records, then inspect all the buses inside and out. Preparing for their visit was a major ordeal. CHP had the power to place buses out of commission. They could even shut down my terminal if we didn't pass. I was always well prepared for them, and PartyLounge passed every year. The CHP turned me into a bookkeeper and expected meticulous records. What a pain in the ass this was!

For quite some time, I'd been wrongly accused by the California Public Utilities Commission. As I'd find out later through some of my connections, the C.P.U.C. had been taking a very close look at PartyLounge. A jealous neighbor was turning me in and making false accusations against my company.

It turned out the neighbor used to be in the limousine business. When I moved into my neighborhood, I made the mistake of bringing a bus home. I preferred to work on them there. I had a special side yard where I could park and where nobody would bother me. I was completely out of view—unlike the bus terminal, where we shared parking with the general public. People would often come up to a bus and invite themselves in, curious to see what I was up to. Generally, I had no time for visitors. When the neighbor saw the coach drive by, he must have viewed it as a threat to his limousine business. The neighbor turned out to be a high-ranking Masonic Lodge member. With his power and influence, he